George Earl Church

Mexico

Its revolutions: are they evidences of retrogression or of progress? A historical and political review

George Earl Church

Mexico

Its revolutions: are they evidences of retrogression or of progress? A historical and political review

ISBN/EAN: 9783337068837

Printed in Europe, USA, Canada, Australia, Japan

Cover: Foto ©ninafisch / pixelio.de

More available books at **www.hansebooks.com**

ITS REVOLUTIONS:

ARE THEY EVIDENCES OF RETROGRESSION
OR OF PROGRESS?

A

HISTORICAL AND POLITICAL REVIEW,

BY

GEORGE E. CHURCH.

REVISED FROM THE NEW YORK HERALD OF MAY 25TH, 1866.

NEW YORK:
BAKER & GODWIN, PRINTERS,
PRINTING-HOUSE SQUARE.
1866.

⁎ Numerous applications for a pamphlet edition of my "Historical Review of Mexico" have induced me to revise that which appeared in the NEW YORK HERALD of May 25th, 1866.

For a clearer understanding of the subject, many details have been introduced, appertaining to the period from the "Revolution of Ayutla" to the French invasion; for it was during that time that the great principles for which the country had been battling were raising their heads above the revolutionary surges which had so long deluged the land. A supplement has also been added, containing some of the later political developments relative to Mexico.

GEORGE E. CHURCH.

PROVIDENCE, R. I.,
  July 4th, 1866.

MEXICO:

Its Revolutions: are they Evidences of Retrogression or of Progress?

A HISTORICAL AND POLITICAL REVIEW.

PART I.

GEOGRAPHICAL POSITION OF MEXICO—HER COMMERCIAL ADVANTAGES—THE TRADE CURRENTS OF THE WORLD—CLIMATE, SOIL, ETC.—HER REVOLUTIONS ELEMENTS OF PROGRESS—ERA OF THE SPANISH CONQUEST—OCCUPATION OF THE NEW WORLD—GOVERNMENT OF THE VICEROYS—LAWS OF THE INDIES—EDUCATION.

From the peculiar and commanding geographical position of Mexico, there is, perhaps, no country in the world destined to play a more important *rôle* in the history of mankind. Situated midway between supply and demand, she stands like a barrier, interrupting and claiming tribute from modern European civilization on the east and ancient Asiatic civilization on the west. At her western doors she may bathe her commercial enterprise in the products of Japan, China, India, Australia, and all the islands of the Pacific. To the eastward, the vast wave of progressive civilization is fast rolling onward towards her shore, bearing with it the demands for ceaseless activity, and the germs of national development. It is upon her territory that the wave of empire, which has for so many centuries been sweeping westward, reaches the confines of that great sea from whose western shore it parted. Northward she enjoys the immediate contact of the wonderful national progress of the great republic, while to the southward, within easy reach, lie the trade and wealth of South America. There is not a commercial country in the world which she cannot reach by easy water communication and in almost a straight line.

With such a magnificent geographical position, there should spring up great cities and commercial centers upon her territory; for, as commerce advances, it will place her, with reference to the modern trade of the world, in nearly the same position that Syria, Mesopotamia, and the whole of Western Persia occupied to its ancient trade. It was the East Indian and European trade currents, flowing over these countries, which gave birth to the cities of Selucia, Palmyra, Sidon, and her colony, Tyre. The same causes, later, forced into notice Byzantium and Alexandria, made Rome and Carthage centres of distribution for East Indian products, and gave Venice wealth and power to turn back the Ottoman sword from Europe.

No better illustration of the importance of occupying a central position, with reference to the great trade currents, can be selected than by the comparison of Europe in the latter part of the fifteenth with the beginning of the sixteenth century. In 1498 her whole Indian commerce flowed westward from its Asiatic sources through the old laborious channels to the eastern shore of the Mediterranean, where the merchants of Genoa and Venice became its principal European distributors. Every Mediterranean port resounded to the hum of commercial life. Suddenly the tide was turned; Vasco de Gama, retracing the track made by Pharaoh Necho's Phœnician ships twenty centuries before, rolled away the barriers to great commercial development, and ordered Europe henceforth to look to the Atlantic coast for centers of East Indian supply. The whole Atlantic seaboard immediately sprang to meet the demands made upon it, and to reap the civilizing influences caused by an intense forcing of mental activity to supply the wants of rival commercial interests, and gather the new harvest laid at the feet of Western Europe. It was like a desert simoon to the Mediterranean ports; the great Nile of Asiatic commerce, which had annually borne in its tide the segregated wealth of the Indies, had changed its course, and now poured its wealth around the Cape of Good Hope and through the dreaded portals of Hercules. The Mediterranean ports which had throve upon its bounty suddenly sunk into mere local importance; or, no longer imbibing its fructifying power, became, like Venice, a mournful wreck of their former splendor. The world now breathed westward. Wafted in its breath, the great trade currents are now fast settling their foci upon the northern half of the New World, and point unerringly to a culmination in Mexico; for, as they have advanced westward, constantly nearing the great source of supply, and constantly having more demand to the east of them, the cities with which they have been pregnant have risen to opulence and grandeur in proportion to their ability to intercept and distribute the waves of wealth flowing past them.

Mexico, so favorably situated, must then have at her command more elements than any other country ever before possessed for the building up of a mighty people. Under the colonial rule of Spain, the advantages which she possessed for a direct trade with the Indies were not overlooked, and her splendid harbor of Acapulco, upon the western coast, became the great center of East India commerce, not only for all the Spanish-American possessions, but even for the mother country, who found it to her advantage to ship direct to the Indies, from the Mexican mines, that silver which the Asiatics so largely demand in exchange for their products; while, from Acapulco, many of the East India goods, crossing the country by the great national road to Vera Cruz, were reshipped to supply the demand in old Spain.

Added to the blessings of geographical position, there is, internally, no country in the world which surpasses Mexico in the natural blessings of climate, fertile soil, and opportunities for the development of agricultural, pastoral, and mineral wealth. While under a united people her military position would be almost invulnerable. Thus preëminent among the countries of the world, she occupies a superior position for great national development, homogeneousness, and intense concentration of the elements of stability.

In making this statement we are not unmindful of the refined horrors entailed upon her by Spanish misrule, nor its zealous cultivation into still more bitter fruit by the Mexican clergy: it is this which has prevented her from making use of those magnificent advantages which Heaven has conferred upon her. Mexico has been too much derided by the world for her misfortunes. Our countrymen are too fond of having her painted writhing under the miseries from which for a half century she has been trying to shake herself free. We have been too willing to compare her woes with the happiness of our own country, which was born under different circumstances; for, while everything aided us in our national advancement, she drank the bitterest dregs that were ever poured out for the mental crushing of a people.

But, in speaking of her chances in the great march of nations, we are looking into the future, when this Mexican chaos shall have cooled down, and the volcanic elements so rudely stirred to action by her priesthood shall find outlet in more peaceful pursuits; when that great cloud of fifteenth century darkness which found its Spanish-American focus in Mexico shall be swept away by the advancing sun of modern civilization, and her people, freed from the incubus of a long night of bigoted religious misrule, may really develop their unexampled opportunities for national prosperity.

The insurrectionary outbreaks which have so long desolated the Spanish-American countries are necessary to their progress in the direction of civilization; at each new revolt, some grievance, some curse which the rule of old Spain inflicted upon them, is thrown into its grave, and the next uprising buries it completely. No one who has not lived in Spanish-American countries and studied their colonial history, can judge of the depth of the flood of entailed woes in which they have had to float their republican arks for a half century, until the subsiding revolutionary surges might give them some hope of rest. Nor does history present instances in European progress where so much misrule has been shaken off so quickly.

In all the Spanish-American republics, it will be found as a rule that, in proportion to their distance from Mexico, the great center of Spanish-American Catholic power, so has been their progress in civilization since their war of independence; for the great prime causes, especially in Mexico, of the numerous revolutions, have been the attempts of the progressive portion of her people to shake themselves free from the crushing rule of the clergy. But circumstances far back in the history of Spain, and having more direct and powerfully drawn lines of cause and effect than most historical events, conspired to turn Spanish character into a tide that spent its full and culminating force upon the American colonies.

Spain, at the very date of the discovery of America, was taking breath after the most terrible religious war on record. It had taken nearly eight hundred years for the flow and ebb of the Moslem tide, and in that time the whole nation had received an intensely concentrated religious education in a single given direction. Spain was the great battle-ground, the bulwark of Catholicism against the more tolerant Moslem faith, whose cimeters, having carved their way across her territory, were threatening to rest on the plains of Italy, under the shadows of the Moslem standards which were advancing westward. Spurred on by all the fiery fanaticism which the Catholic faith could inspire, the whole nation lost itself in a single idea, and became the mighty exponent of Catholic militant power in western Europe. As war rolled on, and shock after shock baptized the Cross in Moslem blood, the mind of Spain lost its balance; every element of the intellect was forced into the channel of religious fervor, until Spain became educated to engraft upon her moral code the most revolting crimes.* Religious fanaticism, true to its instincts to enslave, not to cultivate, the intellect, step by step crushed out every ennobling influence, until the former generosity of Spanish character lost itself in the darkness which advanced southward with their armies. The wild tide, while it hurled back the Moors and drowned human progress in its waves, at length reached the Spanish Jews, who, with all their advancement in civilization, refinement, and wealth, bent to the blast which seemed to drive civilization to the shelter of the Crescent. At length came the Inquisition, to enthrone itself upon the ruin, fit sovereign to crush out the last spark of intellectual opposition to religious fanaticism, and in the wild wreck to sway the destinies of a people.

The rulers of Spain were at that time the monks and inquisitors. Their sovereign, the exponent of a religious idea, turned the thunderbolts in his power to the task of the upholding of the Cross and the overthrow of the heretic. The whole country became a vast monastery, in which the stormy elements of the times swayed natures as potent for religion, ambition and avarice as ever figured in history; and all these elements swayed by the Roman pontiff became in his hands the lash with which he scourged Europe. The brain of Spain, at all times powerful in the direction of its education, proved what mighty efforts man can make when his forces are led in a given direction. The period produced some of the most extraordinary men of history, and though we lament the talent which, perverted, flooded all opposition to its inclinations, we can but admire the genius which could spring from such elements and wield such power with so much success.

Suddenly the barriers which had for so many centuries held in check the flood of religious fervor were no more. Swept southward by the fanatical torrent, the Moors had disappeared across the Mediterranean, and Spain was at length free from

---

* "Any one, it was said, might conscientiously kill an apostate whenever he could meet him. There was some doubt whether a man might slay his own father, if a heretic or infidel, but none whatever as to his right, in that event, to take away the life of his son or his brother."—*Prescott's Ferdinand and Isabella, vol. 2, p. 451.*

civilization and the Crescent — the spiritual fervor was at a loss where to vent its fury; the national mind, missing its accustomed recreation, turned its forces wherever the sanctity of the Cross was to be upheld, and found employment under Cardinal Ximenes, in a campaign against the Moors of Northern Africa, or, later still, against Solyman the Magnificent, in Hungary, and the crushing of Protestantism in Germany. But this was not enough for the occupation of all the turbulent spirits to which eight centuries of warfare had given birth. They sighed for a wider field, and as if destiny had fixed the proper moment, the ships of Columbus brought back the tidings of the wonderful New World which was to become a curse to Spain, of the vast fields which were open for the planting of the Cross and the propagation of the faith. The stories of untold treasures to be gained there expanded like wave ripples, and pandering to the cupidity of the mind linked its two most powerful forces, religion and avarice. The brain of Spain became a vast crucible in which the fiery Spanish imagination melted down the wealth of the New World and threw its power into the religious idea that still swayed the nation. The conquest of Mexico by Cortez, the boldest *filibustero* of his time, and the overthrow of the Empire of the Incas by his cousin, Pizarro, with the tide of treasure which immediately poured into Spain, inflamed to a still higher degree the imagination which had been tame in its estimates of results. To the Spaniard the new sun which shimmered in the west was full of opulent empires only awaiting the Cross and sword of some bold adventurer to build a mighty family upon their ruins.

Expeditions launched out in quick succession and headed toward the New World. They were composed of hardy soldiers who had bronzed their faces in the wars of Italy under the great captain, or in the wars of Spain against the Moors; of Hidalgos of all classes; from the noble with royal blood to the "Hidalgo de Bragueta;" and while they drew into their wild excitement much of the best blood of the Peninsula, they also furnished an outlet for much of the most turbulent and unprincipled element of the Spanish population. The first expeditions were generally of a better class than the emigration which followed. The countries being all occupied or apportioned to Adalantados there was left no inducement to men to organize such knightly expeditions as Pedro de Mendoza fitted at his own cost and led to the conquest of the La Plata region in 1534. Mendoza in this expedition agreed to take with him one thousand men, well armed and equipped, with physicians for the sick, and a number of missionaries for the conversion of the Indians. The latter point was particularly insisted upon by the Emperor. Not even the salary of an Adalantado—two thousand ducats per year—was to be claimed by Mendoza. It was, moreover, especially stipulated in his contract that if any sovereign prince should fall into his hands his ransom, although belonging by law to the Emperor, should be divided among the *conquistadores*, deducting only the royal fifth. It was by such contracts as this that the New World was apportioned to the adventurous spirits of the times. To indicate the intense activity of the Spanish mind in the direction of America, it may be stated that, so soon as the terms of the contract were promulgated, crowds of all classes presented themselves. No less than fifty grandees and gentlemen of distinction took part in this expedition. Among them was Don Juan de Osorio, who had gained great renown in the wars of Italy; Don Diego de Mendoza, a brother of the Adalantado, and who was named Admiral of the fleet; Juan de Ayolas, Don Domingo Martinez, afterwards a famous poet; Francisco de Mendoza, major domo of the King of the Romans, and Don Carlos Dubin, foster brother of the Emperor; all volunteers led by the spirit of adventure and the desire of riches. The multitude desirous to embark became so great that it was necessary to sail before the appointed day; and when the account was taken of the number on board the fourteen vessels which composed the fleet, it was found that instead of the one thousand men for which Mendoza had stipulated, there were twenty-five hundred Spaniards and one hundred and fifty Germans, besides the crews of the vessels.*

It did not appear to be the policy of Spain to found agricultural dependencies. The New World, in its earlier developments, was considered a vast treasure-house of the precious metals. The expeditions of Hernando Cortez and Francisco Pizarro had demonstrated the truth of the theory, and Spain acted upon this principle, expecting in return for her expeditions not agricultural but mineral products. Wherever agricultural settlements were formed, as on the banks of the La Plata, they were the results of the disappointed hopes of the *conquistadores*, who, failing in their attemps to realize their golden dreams, had been forced to cultivate the lands around them to sustain life.

The conquest of the country, whether to glut their avarice or religious bigotry, was the prime object; and they carried it onward with a courage and perseverance which the sole exercise of the two most powerful elements of the mind could bring to bear for the object in view. The tide of conquest, after desolating Mexico, swept across the Isthmus of Panama and over-

---

* See Sir W. Parish's Rio de la Plata.

threw the Empire of the Incas. Southward it flowed, bearing all before it, until at Valdivia they found something of the courage in the Araucanian tribes which animated their own swords; and from that day to this the Araucanians, Huelches, Puelches, Pehuenches, and Pampas have held their territory.*

The country in great part conquered, there became no longer any new kingdoms awaiting the adventurous sword; and the problem then was to make the most of the silver harvest which had fallen into their hands, and to see how much precious metal might be produced in the shortest possible time. The wars of Charles V. and Phillip II. demanded that the colonies should produce largely; and between the exactions of the clergy and the demands of the Crown, the colonies were ground into silver, grained through Indian blood. The sway of the earlier conquerers overthrew a civilization in Mexico and Peru which they scarcely replaced during their occupation of the country. Spanish America was wrecked, and like a huge hulk thrown among savages, she was torn in pieces to obtain the metal that held her together. It is mournful to contemplate what a garden she might have been to the mother country had a liberal policy ruled the councils of the nation in its government. What could have been the government of the colonies during that long night of Spanish misrule that it could so brand itself upon them, that after fifty years of revolutionary throes, they have been unable to shake themselves entirely free from the curses which still linger in their valleys and hold the cup of misery to the lips of their people. Humanity might well draw a veil over these woes. It is a sickening tale of horror to run through the three hundred years of sword, bullet, fagot, torture, and famine; but a glance at it is necessary to our views of the leniency with which we should judge the Spanish-American people in their struggles for stable government. In Mexico, especially, everything appeared to conspire to hold her in the depth of physical and mental degradation. Under the Viceroys she suffered all the miseries which bad government at home, administered by unprincipled colonial officials, could deal out to her.

Although the "Laws of the Indies" gave the right to creoles to hold even the highest offices, the law of Charles V. stating "that the discoverers, the settlers and their posterity and those born in the country were to be preferred before all others in the offices of the Church, State, and jurisprudence," yet of the one

---

* The author has had the pleasure of participating in two battles against the banded tribes above mentioned, and can attest to their courage, which has lost nothing of its former energy. We have seen them charge a regiment of modern infantry with rude lances made of reeds, having sharpened pieces of hoop-iron bound to the ends of them with hide thongs.

hundred and sixty Viceroys who ruled during the time that Spain held her colonies only four were creoles or natives of the colonies by Spanish parents; and these four owed their position to an education received in the mother country, to which they had added a powerful home influence. Every situation, even the lowest Custom-House clerkship, was held by an European. Of six hundred and two Captain Generals all but fourteen were Spaniards.

The laws were very rigid in reference to the conferring of ecclesiastical benefices upon the descendants of the conquistadores and "pacificators" of the country; but they were so evaded that, notwithstanding the law stipulated that no Spaniard could hold such a benefice, even if appointed by the King himself, yet of five hundred and fifty ecclesiastics who had reached the episcopal dignity in the New World, only fifty-five were natives. The Viceroys,* with rare exceptions, were men whose ruined fortunes and profligate life at home had left them no hope, unless an appointment in the New World might enable them in a few years of its occupancy to return loaded with plundered wealth. Generally, men of the vilest antecedents, court parasites, uneducated and bigoted, they appeared to be selected as crushing machines for colonial silver mines. They were the first to violate the law which allowed the creoles to hold office. The distance to the mother country and the fact that all complaints had to pass through the hands of those who held office were effectual preventives to all redress of this great grievance. At one time, under Godoy's rule of the Indies, every office in the Mexican viceroyalty was publicly sold at auction.

The power of the Viceroy was more than regal. The troops were entirely under his command. Every civil and military appointment was dependent upon him as President of the "Real Audiencia," which controlled all appointments by virtue of the "Laws of the Indies." His salary was $60,000 per year: yet off of this he lived like an eastern monarch and returned home in a few years with a princely fortune. "He reaped profits on the illegal sales of titles and distinctions, granting licenses and the introduction of foreign goods," while "at one time even government situations were in great demand without a salary,"† the opportunities for plunder were so numerous. Special privileges or "Fueros" were granted to Spaniards which enabled them to make vast sums of money. Spanish-America appeared

---

* There were originally but two Viceroyalties, Mexico and Peru. The Viceroyalty of New Grenada was established in 1718, that of Venezuela in 1731, that of Chile in 1734, and that of Buenos Ayres in 1778.)

† See Ward's Mexico.

to be an immense field over which avarice run riot in acts of oppression and misrule.

The *repartimentos* and the *mita* were other evils forced upon the country. The *mita*, as if to grind out every physical effort of the Indian, imposed the most abject slavery. It was a year's personal toil exacted from him; and the owner of every mine had a right to a certain number of Indian workmen, to whom he paid four reals (fifty cents) per day. This was insufficient to keep the Indian and his family from starvation. A system of credit was however established, whereby the Indian could retain life while his physical energies endured, the owner of the mine crediting him with absolute necessities; but if at the end of his term of service he was in debt, the law forced him to remain until it was paid. As it was impossible for him to pay it, the poor Indian found no relief from his misery except in death, which from scanty food, hard labor, and exposure, seldom gave him more than two or three years' lease of existence. The destruction of Indian life was immense; to be detailed to work in the mines was considered by the Indian as a sentence of death. Out of his scanty earnings he was obliged to pay a capitation tax of eight dollars per head, not to speak of the exactions of the clergy, which will be hereafter mentioned. The result upon the Indian element in Mexico was not so crushing as in the other colonies farther removed from the mother country, consequently more liable to misrule; but even in Mexico the philanthropic Las Casas has depicted cruelties which freeze the blood. In the 1,400 mines of Peru, it is stated* that no less than 8,285,000 Indians perished under colonial rule; but this must be an exaggeration. The Indian could not hold property to exceed the value of $50 without permission of the "Protector de los naturales," appointed by the King.

Education, at all times necessary to the intellectual expansion of a people, was confined in the colonies to the narrowest limits. While the rest of the world was basking in the sunshine of a mighty intellectual advancement, while Protestantism was confirming the right to think which God gave to man, the whole of Spanish-America was overspread with the dark veil of bigotry. The curse which had rested on Europe for so many centuries, and from which, after long and tremendous efforts, she had shaken herself free, fled to the New World, where, nursed by ambition, avarice, and all the most fearful elements of perverted human nature, it found a soil where its seeds, planted by the Viceroys and their parasites, and nurtured by

---

* See General Miller's Memoirs.

the clergy, weighed heavily upon the oppressed creole and Indian races.

The only studies permitted in the schools were Latin grammar, ancient philosophy, theology, and civil and canonical jurisprudence, while the only history taught was that of Spain. Public schools were forbidden under plea that "it was not expedient for learning to become general in America." Complete ignorance was the policy imposed. The Board of Trade at Buenos Ayres was not allowed to establish a school of mathematics, it being suppressed by the Viceroy Joaquin del Pino. Juan Francisco, an Opata chief, journeyed on foot to Mexico, a distance of five hundred miles, and crossed the Ocean to Madrid, to solicit the privilege of teaching to his tribe the mere rudiments of education. This petition to the "Council of the Indies" was rejected in 1798. Cirilo de Castella, a *cacique*, failed in a similar cause, which, after a twenty years' effort at Madrid, resulted in his death. Merida, in Venezuela, was, by Charles IV., refused permission to found a university. In Mexico every effort in a similar direction proved entirely fruitless. With the exception of Peru, Buenos Ayres, and Mexico, printing presses were denied to the colonies. In the latter viceroyalty, so late as 1806, there was but one printing press, and that was under the control of the government, to promulgate laws for the crushing of the people and the exaction of revenue.

It is unnecessary to detail the acts committed during this long night of saturnalian horrors which held high carnival from San Francisco to Valdivia. We shall find in the war of the Revolution sufficient human suffering to pander to the naturally morbid condition of the mind which delights in pictures of concentrated misery.

During the long colonial dependence of the Americas, the exclusive policy of the mother country had shut them out from the progress of the Old World; they gained nothing by abrasion with other nationalities; they were free from the heretical doctrines which were rocking Europe like a cradle, and which were giving birth to a new era in the history of religion and civilization. The jealous exclusion of all historical information, except that portion of the history of Spain, which, having passed the censorship of the clergy, was deemed fitted for the colonial mind, had narrowed their ideas of humanity, and entirely unprepared them for the flood of light which was to pour in upon them when the Bourbon dynasty was overthrown in the mother country.

PART II.

INFLUENCE OF CATHOLICISM.—THE CLERGY THE GREAT REVOLUTIONARY ELEMENT.—THEIR IMMORALITY AND EXACTIONS.—THE EFFECT ON THE CREOLES AND MIXED RACES.—BUCCANEERING—THE EFFECT OF THE INVASION OF SPAIN BY BONAPARTE—OPPOSITION OF THE SPANISH-AMERICAN CLERGY TO THE FRENCH OCCUPATION OF AMERICA.—ESTABLISHMENT OF COLONIAL JUNTAS.—SEVERE MEASURES OF THE CADIZ REGENCY.—RESTORATION OF FERDINAND VII.—SAVAGE MEASURES AGAINST THE COLONIES.—APPEAL OF THE COLONIES TO MANKIND.

Catholicism had found a virgin field in America, where it had luxuriated and spread its dogmas, free from all contact with heresies which might contaminate it. The land was free from the seeds of the Eleatic philosophy which the school of Xenophanes, Parmenides, and Zeno had drawn from physical speculations. It was free from the scientific deductions which Aristotle and Zeno had planted in the Old World. The Church of Rome did not have to step into the New World and dash aside such theories as the opening of the Egyptian ports had spread over Europe. There was no contact with extraneous elements; no Pantheism to the east of them; no Greek philosophy; no Mahommedism to overrun some of the fairest territory of the church; no sects to distract the faithful; no Trinitarian controversy to set the mind in action. The religious force which had concentrated itself in the Old World burst over the virgin wilds of the New like a pestilence. The fanatical monk penetrated with the crucifix into the midst of the most savage tribes; while sword, fire, and massacre were the true instruments used in the propagation of the faith, and made more converts than the Bible, whose blessed teachings the Indians received at the point of the sabre. Truly, the sword holds mighty arguments, and, as Mahommedan and Christian have proven, makes more converts than tongue or pen.

In touching the results of the establishment of Catholic power in the New World, we are not attacking the high moral teachings of the Church of Rome, but the perversion of its religion when in the hands of bad men, and its wonderful capacity for such perversion. We know that the Catholic religion was born of the moral wants of the Mediterranean nations, who, completely sunk in immorality, were ready to seize upon any faith which could lift them from the degradation into which the crimes and lust of the Roman empire had sunk them; but, like any other great monopoly of the human mind in a single direction, it soon became perverted, and deemed no measure too atrocious to obtain proselytes. We may not, as Protestants, arrogate too much virtue in our own minds, or proclaim ourselves free from the same religious madness which wrecks what it would beautify. We have only to look at our early history to find acts which are kindred to those of the Inquisition, and that opportunity was alone lacking to make proselytes with quite as much fanatical spirit as was ever used by the clergy of Rome in the New World.

In tracing the causes of the numberless revolutions of the Spanish-American States, we shall find that at every phase of their history, and especially in Mexico, the clergy have been the great vital principle which has occasioned the chronic revolutionary condition of the country. To form an idea of their power, it is necessary to glance at the immense influence which they exercised in colonial affairs, and the vast accumulations of wealth which, by every art avarice could suggest, they wrung from Spaniard and native. There were in Mexico, in 1827, one hundred and fifty convents, besides innumerable parochial churches. The clergy collected, by the exaction of tithes, one-tenth of the whole products of the country. Notwithstanding the tithe system was abolished in 1833 by the government, many of the devoted adherents of the church still submit to it. It cost Mexico yearly to sustain her clergy $8,000,000; while the estimated value of church property was, in 1860, from $250,000,000 to $300,000,000—about one-third the valuation of the whole country. In the city of Mexico there are five thousand houses, valued at $80,000,000, of which the clergy then owned one-half at least. The income of the Mexican Church, in 1860, was about $20,000,000. In 1805, they held $44,000,000 cash. In 1826 it had been reduced to $20,000,000, part of it having been seized by the Spanish government. $40,000,000 of mortgages on the agricultural districts around Puebla supported the religious institutions of that city, which is still known as the most intensely Catholic in the country.

The clergy had, side by side with Cortez, entered Mexico; and, having the light of the sainted religion constantly before his eyes, the bold conqueror never refused to exchange the consolation of the holy faith for the riches of the Indian. Whether by persuasion or the sword, they were baptized by thousands. The clergy never forgot the injunction of the Pope to require them to embrace the Catholic religion; and, if they were unwilling, "to attack them with fire and sword, and exterminate or reduce them to slavery."

So scandalous was the action of the secular clergy in their intercourse with the Indians, that Cortez wrote to Charles V. to send him regulars instead of seculars. Said he:—" The latter display extravagant luxury, leave great wealth to their natural children, and give great scandal to the newly converted Indians."

The time which had elapsed from the conquest of Mexico to the date of the revolution of Hidalgo, in 1810, had only enabled the clergy to expand their luxurious habits, in the ratio of their constantly increasing wealth, which, as we have seen, has amounted to almost one-half of the entire valuation of the country. Unchecked by any supreme power, they had rioted in the most unbridled excesses, heedless of the example which they set to their proselytes, who, in their ignorance, naturally followed their teachings. They contrived to lay excessive exactions upon everything which might contribute to the moral elevation of the people; and, after the civil authorities had wrung the last drop of treasure out of the physical nature of the creole and Indian, the clergy took them, and in their hydraulic religious press squeezed out the treasure from their spiritual development. There are, however, a few shining examples of probity floating in this sea of moral debasement. Don Antonio Raya, Bishop of Cuzco, gave in charities three hundred and seventy thousand dollars in eight years. The Archbishop of Charcas was held in high repute for his honesty and virtue, while several of the bishops of Peru atoned in part for the misrule of others.

The Viceroy and his satellites exerted every effort to lay the most exhaustive taxes upon every article that might possibly yield a revenue. The whole country was given up to the most wholesale system of robbery that the world ever saw. The exactions laid upon the people naturally begot a carelessness with regard to the future, wherein they could only accumulate treasure to pour into the coffers of their masters, who wielded it both for their physical and mental oppression. In Mexico many a wealthy creole, to prevent the loss of his property by the Inquisition, gave immense sums to the holy orders. The one hundred and seventy-five feast days of the year did not leave the poor Indian time enough to earn the enormous marriage fee, of from fourteen to sixteen dollars, which was exacted from him for the performance of such a service by the clergy. The result was that marriage was the exception, not the rule. It very naturally inaugurated a wholesale system of concubinage, in which the clergy were the principal actors. Every social or family tie appeared to be broken, or, at the date of the revolution, had disappeared in the mad vortex of political and religious immorality, which, like a deluge, had swept over the land. The most brutal passions were uppermost in the Mexican mind. Three great castes—Spaniards, creoles, and Indians—had been established at the occupation of the country, and these had, year after year, taken more marked features, until the woes of the two latter were finally forced to coalesce and form a companionship in misery. The creoles had, at the date of the revolution, been ground down in proportion to the jealousy which their constantly increasing numbers had excited in the breasts of the old Spaniards, who saw, from the groans which their intolerable exactions and cruelties had forced from them, that they could not be kept much longer from sharing in the government. The Europeans had heaped woe upon misery, until Spanish-America could no longer endure it. Petition after petition was laid at the foot of the throne; but, spurned in the most outrageous language, they were returned unconsidered to the colonists. A few of the very lowest offices in the Americas had been doled out to the creoles. So late as 1785 the Minister Galvez referred to the fact that a few Mexicans held office in their country as an abuse. Thus was a wide breach opened between the old Spaniard and his progeny. So late as 1817 it was asserted, in a Spanish legislative assembly, that "so long as a man lived in Spain, every American owed him allegiance." And the Oidor Bataller had a favorite maxim, "that while a Manchego mule or a Castilian cobbler remained in the Peninsula, he had a right to govern the Americas."

The effect of this policy upon the creoles, who, at the date of the revolution were very numerous, was most disastrous. Ignorant, though possessing great natural talent, their whole mind had been so warped by the enslaving rule to which it had been subjected, that thought flowed in its channels more by instinct than by reason. With minds corrupted by their masters; with the most disgusting vices engrafted upon their political upas tree; with the clergy pandering to every known vice of a corrupt education; in the culmination of three centuries of the vilest excesses; with honor a myth, virtue a mockery, and honesty buried deep in the foul pool of crime and horror, which seemed to have poured down upon them in a ceaseless torrent, they drank from this sea of misery, until nature, overloaded, shook itself free by revolution.

Following the ideas which were traced out in the action of the Europeans, the creoles imbibed the spirit of their oppressors, and deemed that the only honorable employments were to be found in the army or in the church. In the latter, it had been the policy of the royal government to cherish its temporalities;

and thus the "mayorazgos," or rights of primogeniture, frequently forced the younger sons into the religious orders; but after the right of primogeniture was abolished, during the revolution, the church became unpopular as a profession, except for the lowest classes. We shall see, in the course of the Mexican revolutions, the results of this action, both in the military and in the church.

The only ports from which the Spanish Americans could have communication with the mother country were Porto Bello and Vera Cruz. It was as late as 1774 before the colonies were allowed to communicate with each other, and not until about fifty years before the revolution that commerce from any other port than Seville, in Spain, could be carried on with the colonies. It was not until 1713 that the ships of any other nation were allowed to touch at any Spanish colonial port. Great Britain, at this date, in her contract to supply slaves, had a very slight trading interest granted to her, but confined to the ships in which the slaves were transported. Not until 1764 did monthly packets, which were Spanish, commence running to Havana, Porto Bello, and Buenos Ayres; and it was not until 1810 that the ports of Mexico were fully opened to foreign trade. Spain not only claimed the exclusive jurisdiction of all the Spanish Americas, but even the surrounding oceans, and it was these claims which gave rise to the disputes between the Spanish Crown and Queen Elizabeth, who held that Spain had no right to the possession of territory which she did not actually occupy. This controversy, in connection with the attempts of the Dutch and English to trade in New Spain, gave rise to the buccaneering expeditions which made the Gulf of Mexico ring with the romantic deeds of the freebooters, the capture of richly freighted Spanish galleons, the plundering of Spanish American towns, the sacking of the richly ornamented cathedrals, and other riotous deeds, which gradually caused the buccaneers to sink into pirates, who then seized upon some of the fairest West Indian ports, and, perching their lookout towers upon the commanding points, were ready at any moment to dart out upon the rich treasure ships of Spain.

On the 29th July, 1808, in the midst of the circling influences which the despotic policy of Spain had produced in the colonies, the news arrived of the invasion of the mother country by the troops of Bonaparte, the deposing of Ferdinand VII. on the 5th of May, 1808, and the resigning to Joseph Bonaparte of all the rights of the Bourbon family to the crown of Spain. It is necessary to trace this phase of Spanish history for a moment. Revolutionary measures opposing the French invasion were immediately inaugurated, and several juntas were established in different parts of the country; these juntas, separately claiming jurisdiction in the colonies, occasioned the greatest uncertainty as to which they owed allegiance: this naturally assisted in shaping the events which now followed. Finally these juntas resolved themselves into the "Supreme Junta of Seville," consisting of twenty-three members, mostly of the nobility. It met June 6, 1808, and proclaimed allegiance to Ferdinand VII., whom they attested had been deposed by the French army, and had been forced to surrender the royal rights of a family which were not in his power to surrender. Meanwhile Joseph Bonaparte had summoned one hundred and fifty deputies, ninety-two of whom assembled and accepted the constitution which Napoleon had prepared for them. This constitution provided that the colonies were to be represented in the general Cortes at Madrid, and enjoy all the rights and privileges of the mother country.

From Ferdinand VII. and the Council of the Indies orders were immediately forwarded to the colonies to transfer to France their allegiance. The emissaries of King Joseph were immediately scattered throughout America to make the transfer more certain, and to receive the submission of the country. The old Spaniards vacillated. Some were at first for accepting the new order of things, fearful of losing their fat offices, but an element had crept into the problem which, though quiet in its action, was nevertheless more powerful than all the others combined. It was for the interest of the Catholic clergy in the New World to oppose the French occupation of the Americas, for the government of King Joseph had threatened drastic reforms in the Church, which would militate powerfully against the monopoly which the clergy of the New World held over the tollgates to heaven. The consequence was that everywhere the clergy opposed the French occupation.—M. de Sastenay, who was sent to receive the submission of the inhabitants of the Rio de la Plata, was imprisoned, and the proclamation of King Joseph was thrown into the flames.

At Caraccas the government officials made every effort to turn the government over to the French, who had heavily bribed them; but the people assembled on the 15th of July, 1808, and took an oath of allegiance to Ferdinand VII. Throughout the colonies the clergy used their influence to instruct the lower classes of people to support the cause of Ferdinand; and these raised immense sums and forwarded them to Spain to aid the dethroned King in regaining his crown. Ninety millions dollars were raised for this purpose, and the religious enthusiasm became so great that many colonists crossed the ocean to fight in the ranks of the revolutionists. But the moment had arrived for which the Americans had long hoped, and though loyal still, they seized upon it to advance their social position. Efforts were made by the creoles to disseminate through the masses the idea of their importance and the value of independence. The moving force was the desire to shake themselves free from the dominating hand of the Europeans, but not to separate from the mother country, providing they could have equal rights with the old Spaniards. The interests of the clergy coinciding for the time, the moment appeared most propitious. Loyalty was, however, a strong element in the creole character, and it will be noticed that they made every effort in favor of their Sovereign before the action of the "Supreme Junta" and Cadiz Regency forced them to declare their independence of the mother country.

The period which had elapsed from the first news of the French invasion of the Peninsula until 1810, was all quivering with the agitation of the elements which, in the colonies, had been so long subject to the control of the few. They maintained themselves in complete uncertainty as to their future, and the whole political forces of the country being unsettled, left the people to imagine the wildest theories with respect to their future government. It was in this condition that they received news of the dissolution of the Supreme Junta of Seville, and that some of its members had been accused as traitors; that the French had conquered the whole of Spain, excepting Cadiz, where a Regency had been illegally established by the President of the defunct Junta, who published a decree, without date, naming the five members who composed it.

During this uncertain condition of colonial affairs, the Viceroy of Mexico, José Iturrigaray, more liberal than many of his predecessors, had espoused the popular side and assisted in the formation of a Colonial Junta, which placed him at its head to represent the interests of King Ferdinand during his captivity. But the power of the old Spaniards, who still held the principal offices, both civil and military, was more than a match for the unorganized creole faction, and they, therefore, immediately seized Iturrigaray and forwarded him a prisoner to Seville, where the Junta approved the action, rewarded those who had deposed him, and appointed another Viceroy, Vanegas, who was sent to assume control of affairs in Mexico. It appears that the Supreme Junta of Seville not only claimed full control of all Spanish affairs during its existence, but endeavored to assume control of all the affairs of the New World, that they might obtain sufficient funds to wage war against the French and drive them out of the Peninsula. They were, therefore, bitterly opposed to the establishment of provisional governments by the different viceroyalties, and took measures by every method in their power to prevent such proceedings, proclaiming as rebels all who engaged in their organization.

The Regency which had been organized on the 29th of October, 1810, decreed a very democratic constitution, infringed seriously upon the religious influences of the Church, and abolished the Holy Tribunal. The effect of this upon the New World was to bind the clergy more firmly in their opposition to the Regency, and the support of the colonial juntas, which gave more hopes of a continuance of religious monopoly.

The old Spaniards, who had so monopolized colonial offices, were generally excluded in the formation of the colonial juntas. In Buenos Ayres they were wholly so; but in Chile Spaniards and creoles joined in the general movement until the former, attempting to restore the old order of things, were entirely excluded from the Junta there established. The Spaniards, at first inclined to espouse the French cause, found that in opposition to the creole and church interests, it was impracticable; they, therefore, with the hope of continuing their monopolies, espoused the cause of the Cadiz Regency which threatened to overthrow all the colonial juntas, and restore America to its former dependent position. The native element had, however, grown too powerful to be treated with impunity; the avalanche of free thought and action had received its impetus, and was destined to roll through the land crushing out all attempted opposition. The people had tasted the waters at the spring of power, for which they had so long sighed, and though the fountain has often, from that day to this, flowed blood instead of water in its attempts to free itself from the poison of colonial rule, liberty and progress are still the moving forces of the Spanish-American mind.

The first impulse of the Cadiz Regency was to deal liberally with the colonies. On May 17, 1810, they declared them open to free trade in all articles of their own production which Spain could not consume. The merchants of Cadiz, all-powerful in their monopoly of the colonial trade, found means to have this decree revoked one month after its issue; and the Regency went back to the old system of trade throughout America. It was too late to exercise such a vacillating policy; the colonists had discovered their rights and were now determined to assert them, while, from reasons already mentioned, the clergy sided with them.

It is a notable fact that the revolution in Spain against French power was incited principally by the parish priests, while the nobility and higher orders were the principal adherents of King Joseph. There was a similar power existing in

America; the "Curas," who were in immediate contact with the lower classes, swayed their minds in any desired direction, and the lower orders of the clergy, being composed entirely of creoles and mixed races, naturally exercised their influence in the direction of the provisional juntas from which they had so much to hope.

Strong in the belief that by provisional governments they might be enabled to hold the country for Ferdinand VII., they established juntas almost simultaneously in all parts of the country: At Caraccas, 19th April; Buenos Ayres, 25th May; New Grenada, 3d July; Bogota, 20th July; Carthagena, 18th August; Chile, 18th September, and Mexico, 16th September, 1810.

No people in history were ever blest with a more favorable opportunity to free themselves from the crushing despotism that weighed upon them than were the Spanish-Americans. Their whole country contained but very few Spanish troops. In fact so convinced was the mother country of the loyalty of the colonies that immense districts had been guarded with but the shadow of an army.

When the Regency received news of the formation of colonial juntas, they were animated with the utmost fury against the colonists. They immediately dispatched a royal commissioner to Venezuela, who was "to assume the regal power to its fullest extent; to remove, suspend, or dismiss the authorities of every rank and class; to pardon or punish the guilty at pleasure; to use the moneys belonging to the royal treasury," &c. The Junta of Caraccas refused to receive him. Venezuela was then declared in a state of blockade, although there was not a ship to enforce the decree.

With money which the colonists had furnished the Regency to uphold the cause of Ferdinand VII., an expedition was immediately organized and sent to Venezuela. The whole proceedings of the colonies were declared revolutionary, and instructions were given to the Spanish forces to devastate the country with fire and sword. So thoroughly were the orders carried out that they often murdered their own brothers and relatives whom they found among the insurgents. General Calleja in a dispatch informs the Viceroy that, after losing one man killed and two wounded, he put five thousand betrayed Indians to the sword, and that the total Indian loss was double that number. Most of them were killed while on their knees begging for mercy.

Caraccas capitulated to the Spaniards under General Monteverde, July 25th, 1812. It had been conceded that life and property should be held sacred. An English naval commander

on that station thus describes how that treaty was kept:—
"Monteverde caused to be arrested nearly every creole of rank throughout the country, chained them in pairs, and had them conducted to the prisons of Laguayra and Porto Cabello, where many perished from suffocation and disease." The same officer states that Boves and Rosette, royalist officers, in traversing the route from the river Orinoco to the valley of Caraccas, more than four hundred miles, left no human being alive of any age or sex, except such as joined their standard.

Upon the restoration of Ferdinand to the throne, through the efforts of the English and the defeat of the plans of Bonaparte throughout Europe, he threw himself into the hands of the most bigoted and fanatical of the reactionary party, and refused to uphold the liberal constitution to which the Cortes had taken oath in March, 1812, and in which the colonies were placed upon a footing with the mother country, being entitled to one representative for every seventy thousand inhabitants. He immediately declared the colonies to be in a state of mutiny, refused to listen to any representations from them, but offered to them unconditional pardon. The Viceroys and all their acts were confirmed; the colonists were censured for presuming to frame a government for themselves, and active measures were taken to return to the old system under which they had so long groaned. Large reinforcements were dispatched to America, and in the name of Ferdinand de Bourbon the whole land was made desolate. Morillo, in 1816, entered Bogota, and wrote to Spain that "by cutting off all who could read and write he hoped effectually to arrest the spirit of revolution." Six hundred of the first people of the city were hanged or shot in cold blood. A liberal policy in the royal council would have immediately restored the colonies to Spain, but this course was only widening the breach.

Great Britain interposed her good offices to mediate between the colonists and the mother country, but fruitlessly. Scaffolds were erected on all sides; the sword found wild work; the sanguinary tide of Spanish vengeance had been loosed, and threatened to inundate the whole country. It was in the midst of these wild throes that Spanish-American independence was to be born, and it was from these horrors they were to consolidate their nationalities by fifty years of subsequent revolutions, which were the results of the curses thus entailed upon them. The colonists had poured out their blood and treasure to restore Ferdinand to his throne, and he now rewarded them with chains and massacre. But the revolution in the creole mind had progressed too far, and Spain had no power to again enchain completely the mind which had caught sight of freedom.

To relate the condition of one section is to recount the horrors of all. The Congress of the La Plata, in their address to the nations of the earth, which was more like the "Groans of the Britons" for protection from the savages, said:—" The Spanish Ministers issued vigorous orders to all their generals to push the war and to inflict heavier punishments.' * * *
"From that moment they endeavored to divide us by all the means in their power, in order that we might exterminate each other. They propagated against us atrocious calumnies, attributing to us the design of destroying our sacred religion, of setting aside all morality and establishing licentiousness of manners. They carried on a war of religion against us, devising many and various plots to agitate and alarm the consciences of the people—by causing the Spanish bishops to issue edicts of ecclesiastical censure and interdiction among the faithful; to publish excommunications, and, by means of some ignorant confessors, to sow fanatical doctrines in the tribunal of penance. By the aid of such religious discords they have sown dissensions in families, produced quarrels between parents and their children, torn asunder the bonds which united man and wife, scattered implacable enmity and rancor among brothers formerly the most affectionate, and even placed nature herself in a state of hostility and variance." * * * "They have shot the bearers of our flags of truce." * * * "They have shot many in cold blood after they have surrendered." * * *
"In the town of Valle-Grande they enjoyed the brutal pleasure of cutting off the ears of the inhabitants, and sent off a basket filled with these presents to their headquarters. They afterward burned the town, set fire to thirty other populous ones in Peru, and took delight in shutting up persons in their own houses, before the flames were applied to them, in order that they might there be burned to death." * * * "They have divested themselves of all morality and public decency by whipping old religious persons in the open squares, and also women bound to a cannon, causing them previously to be stripped and exposed to shame and derision." "They have plundered our coasts, butchered their defenceless inhabitants, even without sparing superannuated priests; and, by orders of General Pezuela, they burned the church of the town of Puna, and put to the sword old men, women and children, the only inhabitants therein found. They have in a most shameful manner failed to fulfill every capitulation we have, on repeated occasions, concluded with them."

The Cortes of Spain decreed, April 10, 1813, "That it was derogatory to the majesty and dignity of the national Congress to confirm a capitulation made with malignant insurgents."

This was to annul the capitulation of Miranda, in Venezuela, in 1812.

Such was the rule of Ferdinand from Northern Mexico to the La Plata. The result was that Spanish-America found no opening for herself except to press onward and resist the power that would again enslave her, and they therefore made mighty efforts in the cause of liberty. Our efforts in the United States during the War of Independence pale before those of the Spanish-American States to shake off the curse which weighed so heavily on every hope. Linked in a common cause and animated by a common misfortune, their efforts were not confined to their own States; they marched their armies from Buenos Ayres, under the heroic San Martin, to Chile; from Chile to Peru, over the deserts of Atacama; through the mountain paths of the Andes, trailing their worn forces through the mountain torrents, or lying down to sleep upon the frozen snows of the Cordilleras. Their armies fought and bled as heroically as ever patriot could dream until the battle of Ayacucho virtually closed the contest.

As before stated, the events that we have detailed had a general bearing throughout Spanish America. The crushing policy of Spain was applied to every foot of territory which she held on the Western Continent. In Mexico the problem of liberty was, however, of more difficult solution even than in South America, for reasons we shall now state.

PART III.

Revolution of Hidalgo—Convening of a Mexican Congress—Change in the Policy of the Clergy—They Espouse the Insurgent Cause—"Plan of Iguala"—Conflict of Party Interests—Iturbide Proclaimed Emperor—Mexico under Republican Institutions—A Revolutionary Period—Only Three Systems of Government—Review of the Situation of Spanish America prior to the French Invasion—The Upward Struggle of the Colonies—Mexico during this Period to the Revolution of Ayutla—Alvarez and Comonfort's Administrations—Attempts, under Santa Anna, to Establish a Monarchy—Assembly of a National Congress—Swearing of the Constitution of 1857—Comonfort Deserts the Cause—Siege of the Capital—The "Law Lerdo."

On the 10th of September, 1810, an uprising of the Indians and mixed races took place. It was called the revolution of Hidalgo.* It caused a variation in the Mexican revolution against Spain, which made an essential difference as to the time required by Mexico to free herself from the miseries with which Spanish rule environed her. The revolution of Hidalgo was essentially an outbreak against the oppression which had borne heavily upon the Indians and mixed races. The civil commotions in Spain h,ad so disturbed the rule of the Viceroys that the Indian element had easily observed its importance in solving the problem of future government. It was thus easy to incite them to insurrection. Hidalgo, a "cura," moved by public and private wrongs, headed the uprising, and organized a force of 100,000 Indians and mixed races. The whole success of the movement depended upon the creoles, who then formed a large part of all the regular forces of the royalists. Had they sided with the Indians, the revolution would have been successful and the country freed from Spanish tyranny. Unfortunately for the Indian cause, the first body of insurgents fired into the creole troops, and commenced in the towns an indiscriminate massacre of both Spaniards and creoles. This united the two latter for mutual defence, and for a time the most ruth-

---

* Hidalgo was a creole of extraordinary natural and acquired talent. The great uprising of the mixed races which he organized was to break forth November 1, 1810, but was, by the betrayal of the cause, precipitated, and commenced prematurely on the date we have mentioned.

less barbarities were committed. The Church opposed the insurgents, and the Archbishop of Mexico excommunicated their whole force in a body.*

At Guanaxuato, which Hidalgo stormed and sacked, the most terrible retribution was taken upon their oppressors, and for a time it appeared that the entire pure European blood would be forced from the country. Had the insurgents been properly commanded, there is no doubt but they might have swept every European from Mexico; this, with a lack of the necessary material of war, rendered it comparatively easy for the regular forces to overthrow them.

This terrible war of caste was waged with savage ferocity on both sides. General Calleja met the insurgents and defeated them at Guanaxuato, where he put fourteen thousand men, women, and children to the sword; for which he was created "Mariscal de Campo" for distinguished services, decorated with the Cross of the Order of Charles III., and appointed to the vice-royalty. Hidalgo, through the treachery of Bustamente, was captured and shot July 11, 1811. The insurgents, however, continued the revolution under General Morelos, formerly the lieutenant of Hidalgo, who called a National Congress, which met September 13, 1813, and on the following October declared Mexico independent. This Congress promulgated the "Constitution Apatzingan" October 22, 1814.

Gradually the creoles began to take sides with the insurgents, and very many valuable officers were added to their ranks by the desertions from the royalist forces; but it was not until 1820 that any considerable movement took place among the creole forces in aid of the revolutionists. Gen. Morelos proclaimed that "despots and bad government, not Hidalgo, were the real cause of the insurrection," and the Congress appealed to the creoles to join them in their struggle against the oppression of the dominant class, to join hands with them and overthrow their power. "Brethren," said they, "let us embrace and be happy, instead of mutually bringing disgrace upon our heads." If they could not have peace, they desired to carry on the war in a civilized manner. In article five of

---

* This was a similar uprising to that of Don José Gabriel in Peru in 1780. He was a descendant of the Inca, Tupac Amaru, who was beheaded in 1562 by Francisco de Toledo. The Indians, having endured the most terrible oppression, were roused to revenge themselves upon their tyrants. Undisciplined, without munitions of war, but full of the courage of despair, they for a long time waged a desperate war against both Spaniard and creole. With desperate valor, both men and women fought until Gabriel was made prisoner. As a punishment, "he beheld the execution of his wife and children, and many of his faithful followers; his tongue was then cut out, and wild horses harnessed to his legs and arms tore his limbs asunder."

the conditions upon which they would have peace or carry on the war, they said: "It is contrary to the rights of war, as well as those of nature, to enter with fire and sword into defenceless towns, or to assign by tenths and fifths persons to be shot, by which the innocent are confounded with the guilty; let no one be allowed, under the severest penalties, to commit such enormities as those which so greatly dishonor a Christian and civilized people." They also urged the clergy to abstain from calling it a war against the Catholic religion.

The war, after the reception of this message, was waged by Calleja with relentless fury. Almost every insurgent who fell into his hands was sacrificed. The insurgents were forced to retaliate; and, for a time, Mexico was a perfect pandemonium.

Circumstances were, however, fast inducing the Mexican clergy to throw their influence into the scale with the insurgents. The revolutionary troubles which immediately followed the restoration of Ferdinand VII. in Spain, had shown the Church that it had little to hope from the mother country for a continuance of its monopolies. The blind infatuation of Ferdinand, in waging war upon the colonies immediately upon his restoration to power, had prevented entirely any lull in the stormy commotion wherein the colonies might explain more fully the causes which had impelled them to the course they had pursued during the French occupation of the Peninsula. The clergy, seeing in the liberal constitution of the Cortes nothing but the downfall of the Mexican church system, aided in the estrangement of the colonies, and urged onward the policy of complete independence, unless the signs in Spain might become more favorable to their interests.

The Cortes had, in the liberal constitution sworn to by them, declared the Inquisition abolished, and effected numerous church reforms, while all ecclesiastical positions were placed under their control, and decrees promulgated against church property. This was a direct and staggering blow to the Mexican clergy, unless they could escape its effects by freeing the colony from the mother country. The constitution to which the Cortes had sworn was held in abeyance by the revolutionary condition of the country, and the opposition of Ferdinand, until March, 1820. At that time, the Cortes being reinstated, the free constitution was proclaimed and sworn to by the king, who was forced to follow a popular will which he could not control.

So long as Ferdinand had opposed the popular liberal party in Spain, the Mexican clergy clung to his cause with the hope of a reaction to the old system; but when the news reached them of his adoption of the liberal constitution, they immediately threw their whole influence into the cause of the insurgents in an attempt to establish a separate government, with the idea of inviting the bigoted Ferdinand to cross the Atlantic and accept the crown. At this time Augustin Irturbide came prominently into notice. Although a creole he had entirely adhered to the church, and had thus figured in various subordinate positions. In command of a small detachment of the rayalist forces he had carried on an unsparing warfare against the insurgents. As an instance of his cruelty, he states in a dispatch to the Viceroy, in 1814, that "in honor of the day," Good Friday, " he had just ordered three hundred excommunicated wretches to be shot." Upon the clergy changing sides, Iturbide, under their direction, while in command of a small force on the western coast, in 1820, espoused the insurgent cause, headed the forces that flocked to his standard, and marched on the Mexican capital. At the small town of Iguala, he proclaimed the " Plan of Iguala," or the " Constitution of the Three Guarantees." The movement was entirely successful, as most all the movements for the overthrow of any established government have been in Mexico when the clergy have directed the revolutionists. The City of Mexico was occupied by Iturbide on the 27th of September, 1821. Nearly the whole country, under the influence of the clergy, sent in its allegiance. The newly appointed constitutional Viceroy (O'Donoju) at that moment arrived to assume the reins of government. He was forced to acknowledge the independence of the country; and, in conformity with the plan of Iguala, endorse the right which it gave to the house of Bourbon to the throne of Mexico.

The "plan of Iguala," declared on the 24th of February, 1821, breathed progress and liberal government, but contained one element which was more potent than all the others combined, and indicated, not only the secret control which the church possessed in the revolutionary movement of the country, but its determination to carry its power into every department of state, and to virtually rule the country. The plan of Iguala stated:

First.—The Mexican nation is independent of the Spanish nation and of every other, even on its own continent.

Second.—Its religion shall be the Catholic, which all its inhabitants profess.

Third.—They shall be all united, without any distinction between American and Europeans.

* * * * * *

"*Eighth.*—His Majesty Ferdinand VII. shall be invited to the throne of the empire, and, in case of his refusal, the Infantes Don Carlos and Don Francisco de Paula."

* * * * * *

Twelfth.—An army shall be formed for the support of religion, independence, and union, guaranteeing these three principles, and therefore it shall be called the army of the "Three Guarantees."

So soon as the army which bore these principles upon their banners had entered the capital, a junta was established, of which Irturbide was proclaimed President.

The country breathed a moment after its long struggle of eleven years of internecine strife, which had finally culminated in independence and the establishing of a junta free from foreign control.

Thus the clergy, the creoles, and the Indian and mixed races, had banded their interests and reached the first point in the problem of Mexican freedom. But the moment was pregnant with an intense and fresh mental activity; one step reached, another, perforce, must be taken, and they immediately divided into three parties.

The republicans wanted a central or federal republic, and they opposed the military power, whom they accused of a desire to usurp all authority, which properly belonged to the whole people. The Bourbonists adhered to the idea of inviting Ferdinand to the throne; and, being very strongly supported by the clergy, were really the dominant party. The third party which sprang up was the Iturbidists, who desired to place their favorite upon the throne which the plan of Iguala had reserved for Ferdinand de Bourbon. A larger part of the military, having followed Irturbide in his successes, were in favor of the latter movement. The adherents of Irturbide did not, however, feel themselves sufficiently strong to attempt this movement while the clergy favored the Bourbonists. Thus the growing interests of the different parties daily made a wider gap between them, and daily pointed to the necessity for some strong hand to turn the powerful revolutionary elements into a peaceful channel. In this condition of affairs, news arrived from Spain that the Cortes had refused to ratify the treaty of Cordova, which the Viceroy O'Donoju had signed with Irturbide. It was thus rendered impossible for any Spanish Bourbon to ascend the throne.

In the uncertain position in which the Bourbonists now found themselve they were unprepared to oppose the rapid action of the Irturbidists, who now proclaimed Irturbide Emperor, under title of Augustin I., and forced Congress to ratify the usurpation. Immense sums were voted to maintain the royal dignity, a large army drained the resources of the people, and the Emperor, waiving all constitutional considerations, made himself virtually dictator. His reign was, however, a very short one; the federal party had grown formidable, and pandering more essentially to the interests of the church, issued a "pronunciamiento" which roused the country, won over a large part of the army, and resulted, through Generals Victoria and Santa Anna—the latter of whom here first appears upon the stormy waves of Mexican politics—in the establishment of a representative Congress, in August, 1823, the adoption of a federal constitution in 1824, and the appointment of General Victoria as first President of the republic.

This was the first thoroughly considered and well digested constitution which Mexico had. It was, moreover, acknowledged by the whole country, while that of October 14, 1814, was only adopted by the section under control of the insurgent forces commanded by Morelos. The more perfect and democratic republican constitution of 1857 was to grow from the seeds here planted in 1824.

The Mexican Church was in trouble. The elements of republicanism, following rapidly upon the heels of freedom from Spanish oppression, had crept into the worn frame of colonial misrule, and the intellect of the creoles, expanding with the new lights of education and advancement, forced the clergy to direct the storm they could not breast.

The new constitution, however, still clung closely to that curse upon the body politic which has been so fruitful in revolutionary throes. It provided, in Article 50, for a concordat with the Holy See, which was to throw nearly the whole of the Mexican Church management into the hands of the Roman pontiff. The clergy figured to exempt themselves entirely from any chance of government control over their property and monopolies. The old shadow of caste crept into it; the secular and parochial clergy were confined to the lower offices, such as parish priests. All the bishoprics, deaneries, and chapters could only be filled by old Spaniards. It will be remembered that the lower orders of church offices had been the only ones during colonial rule to which the creoles and mixed races were eligible. Thus the old feeling of caste still shook its head above the soil of Mexico, and, united with the clergy, cursed the land it had already desolated.

It is unnecessary to run through the long list of revolutions which have torn Mexico in her struggles to free herself from her inherited miseries. The numbers of presidents and dictators who have followed each other in rapid succession, shows what a terrible struggle and fratricidal strife has been going on at our very doors for nearly a half century from the date of the revolution of independence.

But in mentioning these numerous changes, it must not be supposed that there were as many parties sustaining different principles: there were never more than three; and the whole country became at last swallowed up in the two great ones—the Church, with its reactionary system; and the Liberals, who opposed it with reforms and innovations. The latter, as we shall see, finally triumphed, when, in 1857, the constitution which they promulgated became the organic law of the land. It was the shock of the contending forces of these parties which threw the presidential power first into the hands of one, then of the other; making the numerous changes in power, which have heretofore been erroneously considered as the result of constantly changing political principles. The three classes of government which have in turn ruled Mexico since her Spanish war of independence, are the empire, the republican federal constitution of 1824, the centralized military dictatorships, and the return in 1857 to the reconstituted federal republican government, under the Liberals who had so many years been advocating it with sword and pen. Since that date there has been another period of centralized military dictatorships, under Zuloaga and Miramon; a return again of constitutional government, under Juarez; and latterly, the attempted usurpation of the government by the French, for the purpose of establishing the imperial rule of Maximilian.

When the viceroyalties of America severed the ties which had bound them to the iron embrace of Spain, they found themselves exposed to the wildest theories of government. It had been less than a half century since they had been allowed internal communication with each other. We have seen that the only political education they had received was the history of Spain; which had for centuries shaped its laws under the shadow of the inquisition. The vast influence of the Jesuits and other orders of the Romish clergy, all tended to the formation of governments in the New World which might crush out every spark of information which had not passed the censorship of the church. The religious bigotry of Spain, which we have seen educating itself in eight hundred years of Moorish warfare, had spread its full force over the colonies, and repelled every ray of civilization which attempted to penetrate the universal gloom.

When communication with the Spanish-Americans was opened, during their war of independence, the people looked across the Atlantic for instruction in government, and they saw—chaos! "Should they be republics?—the French republic of 1793 had fallen. Should they be monarchies?—one of the kings of Spain was an imbecile, the other was a captive. Should they be empires?—the great emperor, as a warning, was bound to the rock of St. Helena."

To the northward they saw the rising glory of the great republic, its wonderful advancement, its power, and peace. No internecine strife resounded through its valleys and covered its people with the symbols of mourning. They are happy! why may we not be happy under a similar form of government? Henceforth the United States became their solar centre; they drank in its brightest rays, and fashioned their constitutional governments upon the model of their great luminary. The material with which they had to deal was crude; it had scarcely reached the eocene period of political stability. The revolutionary vista loomed up darkly before them; but they bravely grappled with the problem, and, with herculean efforts, hurled the States into the planes of their orbits. They had baptized their advent into new life with the blood of their bravest sons; they could have established different and temporarily stable governments, which would have given them rest for the moment, but their bold leaders resolved every malign element into the one great crucible, and, unsheathing their swords, exclaimed, "Here is the problem—we will kindle the fires of revolution over eighty degrees of latitude, but we will melt down these elements which curse us, and although we may not know the exact date of our regeneration, we do know that the exponent of that unknown quantity is liberty, and that we constantly approach it."

The States thrown into the planes of their revolutionry orbits were in their courses most erratic. The sunshine of freedom struck upon a race which had been illy prepared to receive its rays. There were elements in their organization which had driven Europe into the most exhaustive wars of the sixteenth century; battled out of Europe, these elements had taken refuge and rooted deeply into the soil of the New World, and at their first outbreak, showed how bitterly their "Dead Sea fruits" were to act upon the people who fed upon them. Their race had been taught that labor was degrading; that honest toil was a curse to manhood instead of a blessing; that there were but three avenues to honor—first, the Church; second, the State; third, the army. Naturally taking their ideas of action from those who had ruled over and educated them in a single direction for three hundred years, even now, from the highest to the lowest position, they evince but too often that most unrepublican, haughty, and arrogant bearing which it must take long to eradicate. Their best educated men see this, and, in proportion to their education and breadth of views, are free from this defect of character. The old Spaniards had left upon them, too, their habits of plunder and misrule; the effects had to be eradicated. Agricultural pursuits were degrading; they were to be made honorable. The gambling spirit was predominant; it had to be curbed. The laws were of ancient Spanish mould, unsuited to modern progress; they were to be remodeled. France had instilled into them, among the first books which they received, the "red republicanism" and Utopian theories of the French revolution; the effects had to be modified. In a late address before the Rhode Island Historical Society, the learned Minister from the Argentine Republic, Don Domingo F. Sarmiento, said:—"You have not been exposed to the dangerous influence of France from 1810 to 18—, and I know not what, disturbing you with pernicious writings and evil examples, holding up alternately, as the *maximum bonum* of government, first the republic, then the empire, next the restored monarchy, again the popular monarchy, then throwing down the monarchy and restoring the republic, crushing the republic and establishing the empire. You have not had, as we have, a more fortunate republic, such as the United States, as a neighbor, tantalizing you by holding up, as examples, its liberties, its wonderful progress, and its federation."

In a fierce struggle of ten years, the colonies had leaped from the sixteenth to the nineteenth century, and suddenly, in the light of the progress which the nations of the world had made in three hundred years, found themselves dazzled with the efforts which they were forced to put forth to reach the level of modern civilization. They saw that, while the world had been advancing, they, under the iron heel of Spain, had lain dormant; and when they awoke to life and breathed the first inspiration of liberty, they found themselves the Rip Van Winkle of the sixteenth century plunged into the mad race of the nineteenth. They looked around them for the elements with which they were to effect their regeneration, and what did they possess? The whole land was a wild wreck of desolation. Who were their educated men who were to grapple with this giant problem? Alas! education had been limited to the old Spaniards whom their ten years of civil strife had, as the first step toward liberty, forced from the country. The abundant talent which their soil had produced was as untrained as the luxuriant vegetation which runs wild in their tropical districts. It wanted cultivation, and they set about the giant task; but it was in the midst of the civil hatreds which war, famine, and entailed miseries had forced upon them. Where were their teachers? They had none. Where were their schools? There were but a few private ones, and these under control of a bigoted clergy. Were there any public ones devoted to the expansion of the intellectual forces? You might have traveled from San Francisco to Chiloe without finding one.* When schools were organized, to what influences were they subjected? Suppose, at the beginning of the sixteenth century, a school for the teaching of liberal government, the laws of progress, the sciences, and all those great elements of nineteenth century mental development, had been established in Rome, how much military force would it have required to preserve it intact? What anathemas from the Roman Pontiff! what secular power, limited only by ecclesiastical effort, would have trained its ordnance upon the plague spot in their midst, until it would have disappeared, if only by the centripetal attrition of the revolving forces! Yet this is the picture of Spanish-America when it broke from the yoke of Spain; and it has been in the midst of such opposing elements that she has had to plant the germs of that educational advancement which has thus far blessed her efforts. "Liberty," said Rousseau, "is a succulent food, but difficult of digestion." He should have added, when mingled with all the old-time ideas engendered by bigoted opposition to advancement.

Said General Bolivar, in his speech to the Congress of Venezuela, "Morals and knowledge are the cardinal points of a republic, and morals and knowledge are what we most want." So thought and so think all the great men of Spanish-America, and laboring in the task, they still struggle onward, at each revolution sweeping some old curse from the land, and ascending one step higher in the scale of political progress.

Another seed which Bolivar planted in the political soil of Spanish-America was, that "knowledge and honesty, not money, are the requisites for exercising political power." He evidently valued the brain, not for the gilding which enabled it to reflect light, but for its powers of absorption.

Never were human talents put to a severer test than were those of Spanish-America, and especially the Mexican portion, to bring order out of this vast pool of the gathered misrule of centuries; and never have patriots worked harder in a glorious cause than have those of Spanish-America for the regeneration of their land. But amid all the elements which they found

---

* In 1551, there was a university founded in the city of Mexico, and a few schools, supposed to be public, but public only to the privileged classes, were afterwards established for priests and lawyers. An excellent academy of mines and mining engineers gave, to those who could gain admittance, superior advantages in an art so essential to make the Mexican mines productive. All these schools were, however, more or less controlled by the priesthood.

wanting to aid them in their heroic struggle, that of education was the foremost; how to educate the people became the great problem which has to this day agitated the first minds of the country, and which has been fruitful in revolutionary opposition to its progress. The first necessity was to confine within proper limits the influence of the church; and in Mexico, constant hammering at its power for fifty years, although with feeble force, has produced the effect, if only by abrasion, to tear off some of its tentacula, which have been fixed upon every element of progress in the land, and which have spread their slimy curse upon every effort at mental development. Never did a more bitter tide flow over a land than that of the clergy over Mexico. It has thrown surge after surge of revolution from one end of the country to the other in its mad efforts to drown progress, or at least to guide upon its dark tide the elements which it has been unable fully to hurl back. Its vast monopolies of estates have held one-half of the country in mortmain, and have made the whole land a palimpsist, where, age after age, one curse has been rubbed in to give place to the next. What wonder that their land is revolutionary! What wonder if they should take a hundred years to free themselves from this leper spot upon their soil! We, born under a happier sky, and with our religious wars fought out for us by almost a half century of revoluntionary conflict in Europe, should look with more sympathy upon the struggle of a people for religious and civil freedom. Thoughtlessly the great mass of our countrymen point to Mexico and South America and wonder why the political elements are so stormy. The North American child was wafted across the ocean, born of the very essence of German and Anglo-Saxon progress, with its religious wars all fought, its laws all shaped to the times, and carrying with it but one curse —slavery. Even this one last curse has taken four years of the brain, blood, and, though but of slight moment, treasure of the country, to sink it among the dark barbarities of the past. How much time, then, should we give to a people to shake off, at one effort, all the curses herein enumerated? The nursling which the Spaniards brought to the New World was the very concentration of the religious bigotry which had sought refuge in Spain at the end of the fifteenth century. The child wrapped in the swaddling clothes woven in the religious looms of the dark ages of European history, was an exponent, a germ, of all the curses which had surged around the Mediterranean from the Christian era to the time that the light of modern civilization broke in upon Europe. It wore a garment woven by the seven crusades, which, from Marseilles or down through the Adriatic, had stretched across the Mediterranean, or from Cologne or Metz, had, preceded by a goat and a goose, swept through the heart of Europe on the way to the Holy Land. It was wrapped in all the dark mysteries which the clergy of Rome could smuggle out of the light which was at that time breaking in to civilize Europe. Rocked under the upas shade of the Inquisition, it breathed the polluted atmosphere which had been poisoned by the ecclesiastical vengeance born of such massacres as that of Lavaur, and the Church of St. Mary Magdalen. By ten years of savage warfare, Spanish-America unrolled the reeking rags of the fifteenth century, and the light of liberty shone upon the new birth. Warped by all that ecclesiastical fanaticism, linked to Spanish avarice, could concentrate in a single element, it was plunged into the mad whirlpool of our present age, and expected, at a single stride, to attain our level. But to give them but fifty years to attain a point which it has taken us three hundred years to reach, is to acknowledge their mental superiority over us. They want time; their revolutions are absolutely essential to their progress. The Mexican Emperor, Iturbide, in his ostracism at Leghorn, aptly alludes to the false view which has been taken of Mexican affairs. He says:—"Nature produces nothing by sudden leaps; she operates by intermediate degrees. The moral world follows the laws of the physical. To think that we could emerge all at once from a state of debasement such as that of slavery, and from a state of ignorance such as has been inflicted upon us for three hundred years, during which we have had neither books nor instructors—and the possession of knowledge has been thought a sufficient cause for persecution—to think that we could gain information and refinement in a moment, as if by enchantment—that we could acquire every virtue, forget prejudices, and give up false pretensions—was a vain expectation, and could only have entered into the vision of an enthusiast."

In Mexico, up to the time of the revolution of Ayutla, which resulted in the establishment of the constitution of 1857, the Holy Catholic Church has been the main feature in every constitution, and no reform has been attempted wherein the clergy have not introduced a religious element, having a tendency to maintain the fast-rooted bigotry of their spiritual power. Their religious, linked to their moneyed influence, has always enabled them to overturn all the efforts of the liberal-minded, progressive party, who have, however, nobly clung to the task of overthrowing this curse upon their body politic. In 1833 the combinations of the progressionists had somewhat trammeled the clergy, but they, by bloody revolutions, upset the presidents, who followed each other in quick succession, and were enabled, through the aid of Santa Anna, to shake themselves almost entirely free from any State influence. By this the bishops held sole control over all ecclesiastical property, becoming the great bankers of the country, effecting loans, taking mortgages upon all kinds of property, and acting in all respects like immense commercial and moneyed corporations.

In the proclamation of the "Basis of Political Organization of the Mexican Republic," the "Holy Catholic Faith" was the most salient feature. It held in its vicelike grasp the elements of progress, and refused to liberate them. So early as 1824 an attempt was made in the State of Guadalaxera to confiscate the church property; but it was met by a decree from the General Congress, which opposed the measure. Congress, however, passed a law in 1833 abolishing Church tithes, which tax upon the agricultural products of the country had yielded the clergy a large revenue. This decree of Congress, did not, however, have the effect intended, for a greater part of the ignorant people still render into the coffers of the Church the old tax, which their religion teaches them it would be sacrilegious to withhold.

From 1833 revolution after revolution followed in quick succession, each eating into the revenues of the Church. One party trying to grasp at a portion of the Church property that they might rid the country of its curse; the opposition, aided by the funds of the clergy, waging a war to retain the property intact. In 1834, Gomez Farias, one of the first leaders in reform, advocated in the legislative halls the confiscation of the Church property; but Santa Anna, in consonance with his attachment to church interests, opposed the measure. During the government of Farias and Barrigan, in 1835, a fruitless attempt, leading to another bloody war, was made to confiscate this property, and appropriate it to the payment of the public debt. The liberals had, in a succession of wars and presidential overturnings, been gradually gaining ground and encroaching upon the church power, which, although eminently superior in financial resources, still found itself forced to make great effort to hold the ascendency in face of the innovating influences of nineteenth century progress and the advancing civilization which from the United States was constantly impinging upon its border. A law was passed on 7th January, 1847, by Congress, to sell or mortgage a portion of the church property in order to raise $15,000,000 to carry on the war against the United States. It was, however, never executed, owing to the opposition of Santa Anna then in control of the government.

Hard pressed in 1854, the reactionists, through their champion, Santa Anna, still nursed the hope that out of the fecundity of Europe they might receive a royal ruler. Their efforts to effect this had been increasing since the independence of the country. Knocking constantly at the nurseries of the great European royal families, they hoped when success crowned their efforts that their rule, over the land might be confirmed, that the cowl might once more cover the helmet, and the saintly frock conceal the sword. In 1845, under General Parades, they had pressed the Spanish throne for a prince, but though the measure received the secret sanction of Western Europe, the moment was not propitious. But in 1854 the effort was more powerful. Santa Anna, then Dictator, commissioned Gutierrez Estrada, with full powers, "to negotiate in Europe for the establishment of a monarchy in Mexico," saying, " I confer upon him by these presents the full powers necessary to enter into arrangements and make the proper offers at the courts of London, Paris, Madrid and Vienna, to obtain from those governments, or from any one of them, the establishment of a Monarchy derived from any of the royal races of those powers, under qualifications and conditions to be established by special instructions." Though this measure was urged by the clergy with all their influence the effort was unsuccessful; the great Republic of the North was too compact, too well filled with the spirit which the Monroe doctrine had infused into the people to allow it to look calmly on and see Western Europe undertake an armed crusade against republicanism in the New World. The European nations saw that the moment was unpropitious—too dangerous—they waited.

In 1855 the liberals had so far gained upon church power that General Ignacio Comonfort occupied the presidential chair. The ecclesiastical party had made a heroic struggle, but their great champion Santa Anna had, upon their overthrow, been forced to fly from the country. At the moment of his departure, the liberals being at some distance from the capital, an attempt was made by the clergy to organize a government upon a conservative basis, if possible, effecting a compromise with their opponents, vainly hoping to protract their power by delaying the final triumph of the progressive efforts at reform which the liberals were so boldly hurling against them. A similar attempt will doubtless be made by them, in fact, we believe is already in progress, to effect a compromise upon the overthrow of Maximilian.

Urged by the church leaders, General Romulo Diaz de la Vega, who commanded the forces deserted by Santa Anna, attempted to organize a government at the capital. It was a weak military dictatorship of a few days, and scarcely worth the dignity of mention. The plans of the conservatives fully arranged, Carrera was installed as nominal chief, but it was for a month only that he exercised a power which extended not beyond the city limits. The effort was in vain, the liberals soon occupied the capital.

The great movement of this period, therefore, was that of the liberals, headed by Alvarez and Comonfort, against the reactionary or Church party, headed by Santa Anna. General Alvarez, the most prominent in the leaders of the revolution of Ayutla, though from his infirmities taking a less conspicuous part in the campaign, had, on the flight of Santa Anna, convoked an Assembly, October 4, 1855, at Cuernavaca, eighteen leagues south of the city of Mexico. This Assembly appointed him to the Presidency. On the 17th of the same month he issued a proclamation calling an election of Deputies to a National Congress to meet "for the purpose of reconstituting the nation under the form of a popular representative democratic republic." This Congress met on the 18th February, 1856, and after prolonged sessions adopted a constitution which was finally sworn on the 3d February, 1857, and became, what the constitution of 1824 was before that time, the organic law of the land.

The cares of government, old age and infirmities, had induced General Alvarez, on the 12th December, 1855, to resign and appoint General Comonfort "President Substitute." Comonfort was subsequently made President by a formal election under the constitution of 1857, and on the 1st of December of that year, again took oath to defend that great liberal code of laws. Afterwards, under the constant assaults of the clergy, and an empty treasury, which gave him no means to properly construct the Government, he conceived that he was fettered by this code whose great principles he believed he might sustain while he abandoned their legalized expression. He therefore, on the 17th December, 1857, pronounced against the constitution, and, aided by the Zuloaga brigade, attempted by a *coup d'etât* to establish a dictatorship, which he termed a revolutionary government; but he only succeeded in teaching the liberal party a lesson which should never be forgotten—not to permit another revolution within itself.

The reactionists seized the favorable opportunity so unexpectedly offered to them; and, on the 11th of January, Zuloaga and his brigade, instigated and corrupted by the clergy, pronounced against Comonfort, who, too late, saw and attempted to correct his error. He now tried to effect a compromise between the reactionists and liberals for the formation of a moderate party, but both parties throwing him aside, he, on the 21st of January, 1858, abandoned the capital and voluntarily embarked for the United States, leaving to firmer hands the cause he had before done so much towards bringing to a successful issue.

The liberals, in sustaining the reforms embodied in the "Plan of Ayutla," which Alvarez and Comonfort had so successfully supported, had attacked, directly, the Church property through the "Law Lerdo," or law of "desamortization." Under this law, the author of which was Miguel Lerdo de Tejada, a very able and patriotic statesman, who was at that time Minister of the Treasury, the Church was required to sell its lands and houses to such of its tenants as should make application; or, in default of application, to such other persons as should first propose for the property. The sale was to be effected for such a sum as the rent then paid would be the interest upon at six per cent. per annum. This sum was to be placed in a perpetual mortgage, to bear an equal interest, and to be held by the Church. The Government was to receive a tax of five per cent. on the amount of sale; it being a slight increase upon the existing tax on all transfers of real estate. In this manner $18,000,000 of real estate passed into the hands of private individuals who thenceforth necessarily supported the Constitutional Government.

The clergy, however, left no measure untried to prevent its execution; they even refused final absolution and sepulchral rites to purchasers. The law, however, only changed the title of the Church from a fee simple to a mortgage, and was intended to secure an enlarged proprietary and consequent improvement of the estates. It was not sufficiently sweeping, and the tame policy of a partial attack upon the clerical domain was the cause of its non-success at the moment. Naturally, at that period, the minds of the people had not been fully awakened to the importance of the great principles involved, and the effect was a compromise between the more enlightened minds and the conservative portion of the party, who were not fully prepared to accept the tremendous responsibilities which the Constitutional Government under Juarez afterwards assumed in the issue of the sweeping "Decree of Secularization" which was proclaimed at Vera Cruz in July, 1859.

PART IV.

ACCESSION OF JUAREZ TO THE PRESIDENCY—BIOGRAPHICAL SKETCH OF HIS LIFE—CHURCH GOVERNMENT AT THE CAPITAL—THE "LAWS OF REFORM"—THE TERRIBLE THREE-YEARS' CONTEST—FINAL TRIUMPH OF THE LIBERALS—THE LIBERAL AND CHURCH CREEDS—THE CLERGY INTRIGUE FOR A FOREIGN INTERVENTION—THE "DECREE OF SECULARIZATION"—ZULOAGA AND MIRAMON—ACTION OF THE DIPLOMATIC CORPS—MANIFESTO OF THE LIBERAL GOVERNMENT—EFFECTS OF THE FINAL SUCCESS OF THE LIBERALS—THE CHURCH PARTY PLUNDERS THE "BRITISH BONDHOLDERS' FUND"—MEXICO UNABLE TO COMPLY WITH FINANCIAL DEMANDS OF THE EUROPEAN GOVERNMENTS—RENEWED ACTIVITY OF THE CLERGY TO INDUCE FOREIGN INTERVENTION.

By a provision of the constitution of 1857, the Chief Justice of the Supreme Court, who was also Vice-President of the Republic, became President in default or by absence of the President elect. Fortunately for Mexico, Benito Juarez,* a man of

---

* President Benito Juarez is by birth an Indian of the ancient Zapoteco race, which, at the time of the conquest, was one of the most powerful in Mexico. He was born in 1809, in the province of Oaxaca, near the village of Ixtlan.

At twelve years of age he left his father's herds, mingled in the excitement of a country fair, and disgusted with the thought of again returning home, accepted employment in a mule train then *en route* for Oaxaca. At that city he encountered Señor Salanueva, a merchant, who, attracted by the rare natural gifts of the boy, adopted him, and gave him the best education within reach. The youth soon graduated with high honors at the College of Oaxaca; commenced the practice of law, and rose rapidly to distinction. In 1846 he was elected member of Congress, after having occupied numerous honorary positions in his native State. He soon after became President of the Supreme Court of Justice of Oaxaca, and in 1847 was elected Governor of that State. In this position he urged numerous public improvements, infused life into the development of mines and manufactures, and, by establishing numerous schools, gave an impetus to educational interests. In 1852 he filled the chair of Civil Law at the Institute of Oaxaca, and afterward became permanent President of the Institute. At this time, by the advocacy of liberal institutions, he attracted the attention of the reactionary government, then under the Dictatorship of Santa Anna; was exiled, and retired to New Orleans.

The Revolution of Ayutla, in 1854, enabled Juarez to return to Mexico, where, in 1855, he was again elected Governor of his native State. When Alvarez became President, *ad-interim*, after the overthrow of Santa Anna and the Church Party, Juarez became Secretary of State for the Departments of Justice, Ecclesiastical Affairs, and Public Instruction. Under his Secretaryship was issued the law abolishing military and ecclesiastical "fueros," giving for the first time in Mexico equality before the law. After again having been Governor of his native State, he was, in 1856, elected to the National Congress, where he assisted in framing and adopting the Constitution of 1857.

In the first election under the Constitution, the progressive party nominated

sterling integrity, was holding that position at the time of the *coup d'etât* of Comonfort. He refused to join the movement, and was in consequence, with several other officials, imprisoned until it was consummated; but, upon the flight of Comonfort, and just previous to the establishment of the government of Zuloaga, he was liberated, and, with others faithful to the liberal cause, succeeded in escaping from the city. He reached the city of Queretaro, where he immediately issued a proclamation reorganizing the Liberal Government, and calling upon the people to rise to the defense of the Constitution and the principles of reform to which the whole country had taken oath. This was followed by a decree, on February 9th, 1858, declaring all the acts of the so-called Zuloaga Government null and void.

The church party, with Zuloaga for its exponent, had gained possession of the capital by the flight of Comonfort. This was on the 21st of January, 1858. On the 22d, Zuloaga convoked a junta of twenty-eight persons named by himself, who in turn named him President of the Republic. Before the 30th, the machinations of the church and reactionary leaders had induced the representatives* of foreign powers resident at the capital, including even the minister from the United States, to recognize Zuloaga as the legitimate president of the republic. They apparently, either with lamentable ignorance of the great principles involved in the struggle, or else blinded by the misrepresentations of the priest party, completely ignored the real government of the country; which, by the will of the people under the constitution of 1857, was still the ruling power of the land. This action of the diplomatic corps only aided in prolonging the contest, by giving a certain character and importance to the church party before the world which it would have found it impossible to obtain in any other manner at this period. It virtually gave the church a three years' additional lease of contest, and they availed themselves of it to the fullest measure.

The triumph of the principles of the constitution of 1857 it was well known would seal the fate of the vast estates of the church. The hoary old giant now bared all his muscles—brain,

---

Juarez for President, but Comonfort became the successful candidate. He was, however, in November of the same year, elected President of the Supreme Court of Justice, and became, by virtue of that office, Vice-President of the Republic. Upon the flight of Comonfort, Juarez became President. From that date his history is that of the country.

* A good authority, speaking of this diplomatic corps, says: "The French Minister was a Jesuit; the Minister of Guatemala a devoted son of the church; the American Minister, a Southern man, wanted to treat for the purchase of territory and became the dupe of the others; the English Chargé was controlled by capitalists who had played the game of monopoly so long that they thought it could be played forever."

sword, treasure, and spiritual power, lighted the fires of revolution throughout the land. It was to be the last grand struggle of the wounded Hercules; and, by the kindling of every fagot of church wrath and power, it was hoped that in one grand *auto de fé* might be consumed the constitution of 1857, and with it every liberal sentiment in the country. The liberals now hurled every element into the contest against ecclesiastical vengeance; for three years the civilization of the nineteenth century boldly faced the armed spectre of the middle ages, and deluged the valleys of Mexico with the blood which it was hoped would wash out the stains that the maddened power of the clergy had blotted upon the land. For three long years, with varying fortunes, the red tide ebbed and flowed, burying in its death-grapple both bigotry and advancement. The star of hope for Mexico grew dim; but her patriots, begrimed in the battle-smoke of fifty years of civil strife, still held their heads above the surges, now riding the wave now in its valley, but ever hopeful, ever boldly slashing at the monster which had fattened its bloated carcass upon their fair land. Under Zuloaga and Miramon, the forces of the church, well supplied with material of war, waged fierce conflict with the patriots who gathered, half-starved, poorly-clad, and lacking in everything except determination, under the banner of the constitutionalists.

Driven from Queretaro, the liberal government occupied successively Guanajuato, Guadalajara, and finally Vera Cruz. It was here on the 6th April, 1859, while the capital was still in the hands of the reactionists, that the United States recognized the constitutional government under President Juarez as the legitimate government of Mexico. It was also at Vera Cruz, in July, 1859, that the great decrees known as the "Laws of Reform" were promulgated. At this time there were in possession of the liberals twenty-one states and one territory, out of the twenty-four states and territories comprising the republic, besides all the seaports both on the Atlantic and Pacific. The "Law Lerdo" had been repealed by the reactionists, after the flight of Comonfort, and the property, which had been partly wrenched from the grasp of the church, had again reverted to it with all its old powers intact, so far as the jurisdiction of the reactionists extended. But the contest had, at length, through all the conflicting elements which Spain had bequeathed to Mexico, narrowed itself to two great parties, and the country began to see the dawn of a permanent peace. The liberals, gaining ground, took heart, and through difficulties which might well appall less determined patriots, their cause was at length triumphant.

The great victory of San Miguel Calpulalpan, on the 22d December, 1860, where half the reactionist army was captured, with forty pieces of artillery and all its munitions of war, virtually struck the death knell of the church power, and soon after the liberals appeared before the capital.

While Juarez was closely besieging Miramon, in the capital, the clergy prevailed upon France and England to offer their mediation; but it was refused by the liberals, who entered Mexico January 11, 1861. Miramon and other reactionary chiefs fled the country. Juarez immediately proclaimed the revival of the civil and religious reforms of 1857. He dismissed the ministers of Spain and Guatemala, and the representative of the Holy See, M. Clementi—all for machinations in favor of the ecclesiastical party. On the 9th of May, 1861, Juarez addressed the Congress, and proclaimed that from the efforts of the liberals "were born the laws of reform, the nationalization of estates held in mortmain, liberty of worship, the absolute independence of civil and religious powers, the secularization, so to speak, of society, whose march has been detained by a bastard alliance, which profaned the name of God and outraged human dignity."

This was the result of the terrible three years' struggle from 1858 to 1861; but the church still maintained, under Marquez and others, small forces in the field, which committed the most brutal excesses. They distinguished neither between foreigner or native, but upon every one they levied contributions of blood and treasure. It appeared to be their desire to make a pandemonium of the land, the better to induce a foreign intervention, under plea of humanity to a people whom they were crushing under their bloody despotism. To the sunshine which lighted the land from the banners of the liberals the church opposed the dark creed which, forced into the Atlantic by the civilization of Europe, had swam the ocean and sought refuge in its last stronghold, Mexico.

Look! here is the contrast between the nineteenth and fifteenth centuries:—

LIBERAL CREED OF REFORM AND CIVILIZATION.

Constitutional government in place of dictatorship.
Freedom of religion.
Freedom of the press.
Nationalization of church property.
Army subordinate to civil power.
Free and full opening for colonization.

REACTIONIST OR CHURCH CREED.

Inviolability of church property, and re-establishment of former exactions.
The military and clergy responsible to their own tribunals.
Roman Catholic the sole religion.
Censorship of the press.
No immigrants except from Catholic countries.
A central dictator, only subject to the church, or, if possible, the restoration of a monarchy or a European protectorate.

Such was the political condition of the country when, in 1861, the constitution of 1857 again became dominant, and hope shed her cheering ray over the whole land; but the mighty power of the church was not dead, although the liberals had confiscated a goodly portion of its estates. The clergy, upon their overthrow by the liberal party, had sent their ablest emissaries to Europe to represent the evil condition of the country, and to instill into the monarchists of the Old World the idea that Mexico was hopelessly given over to anarchy. Similar representations to the French Government in 1839—about the time of the French naval expedition against Mexico—brought forth in France a pamphlet which stated that "it is known that it is to the clerical party that the differences which have arisen between France and Mexico must be attributed. This party wishes to bring back Mexico to monarchical rule, and has pushed it to a war with us in order to arrive at this end."

"The priest party thought that by injustice, insult, and outrage, it would bring France to undertake the conquest of the Mexican republic, and that a monarchy would then be established." How well those words, written in 1839, apply to 1861, the whole history of the late French invasion proves.

The preamble of the "Decree of Secularization," issued at Vera Cruz, July, 1859, stated: "That if at any previous time there was room for any one to doubt that the clergy has been a steadfast obstacle in the way of the establishment of the public peace, to-day all men recognize that it is in a state of overt rebellion against the sovereign authority."

"That in misapplying the legacies and gifts which the pious have intrusted to them for sacred objects, the clergy turn them to the public destruction by sustaining and rendering daily more sanguinary the fratricidal dissension which is set afoot in disowning the legitimate authority, and denying that the republic could constitute itself into any form that the majority selected."

In an explanatory circular from the liberal cabinet, the government stated its objects to be:

"To bring to a definite close this bloody and fratricidal war, which a portion of the clergy has for a long time been fomenting in the nation, with the single object of preserving its interests and prerogatives which it derived from the colonial system, thus shamelessly abusing the influence which the riches deposited in its hands affords it, and abusing the offices of its sacred ministry; and, in order to disarm once for all that class of elements which serve as buttresses to support its mischievous sway, the government hold it to be indispensable:—

"1st. To establish, as a general and invariable rule, most perfect independence between affairs of state and those purely ecclesiastical:

"2d. To suppress all corporations of regulars of masculine sex without any exception, secularizing the priests now embodied in them:

"3d. To extinguish equally the associations, archicofradias, brotherhoods, and in general all corporations now existing of a religious character:

"4th. To put a period to the novitiates in the convents of monks, retaining those actually existing in them, with the means and endowments each possesses, and assigning the necessary means for the maintenance of service in the respective temples:

"5th. To declare that all property, &c."

We dwell somewhat at length upon this period in the history of Mexico, for it is the time at which the plant of a fifty years' revolutionary growth was budding into the civilizing reforms incorporated into the measures which sprung from the Revolution of Ayutla, the constitution of 1857, and the Laws of Reform, including this Decree of Secularization. The grand principles found in these had at length reached the surface; but the sturdy plant had yet to face another fierce blast, and this time from Europe.

The clergy, as a last resort to overthrow the liberals, sought the shadow of the French throne, and hoped still to write the doom of Mexico with a quill plucked from the Austrian eagle. The great military and political leaders of the Church party, ostracised by the liberals, filled Paris with false representations of their country. Miramon and Almonte, with others of the Church party, who were the very exponents of the Mexican revolutionary woes, and who had scourged the country with fire, rapine and murder, hovered around the Tuileries; and their plans falling upon willing ears were soon perfected. M. Lefevre, in a letter to the London *Daily News*, January 4, 1864, ably details the tyranny of the reactionary party during the occupation of Mexico by Zuloaga and Miramon. First came two decrees annulling the alienation of church property, and restoring the ecclesiastical and military jurisdiction as it existed before 1853. M. de Gabriac, French Minister to Mexico, was quite prominent at that time in rendering assistance to the reactionary party, for in a letter of February 27, 1858, he recalls to the Archbishop of Mexico the services which he has rendered to the country and to the Holy Church of that ecclesiastical province. "M. Zuloaga, the intimate friend of MM. Gabriac and Otway, had contented himself with imposing a tax upon capital of £1,000 and upwards."

February 7, 1859, M. Miramon, another, and not less intimate friend of these gentlemen, had attacked (and as usual as an "extraordinary" measure) personal property of £200 sterling and upwards, and had included the liberal and industrial professions in the impost. In May of the same year he had imposed ten per cent. on real property. Then came the "Peza" law, or collection of a year's taxes in advance. Then, when it was found that all the financial measures were insufficient to fill the void of the Danaides sieve, which was called at that time the "Public Treasury," the same Miramon taxed all at once, March 20, 1860:

First. Effective capital of £200 and upward.

Second. The liberal and industrial professions.

Third. "Moral capital," or tax upon the wages of employees.

The amount of taxes, which had been tripled by Zuloaga in 1858, was quadrupled by Miramon in 1859, and in case of some Europeans—mostly French, whose minister would not interfere—was sevenfold.

The way that Miramon happened to succeed Zuloaga was peculiar, both being of the reactionary party. In 1858, Zuloaga had issued his "Christmas pronunciamiento"—the harpies of desolation had been quarreling about the spoils. The country had to be pacified, and under plea that the government of Zuloaga lacked authority, they for a moment conferred it on Robles, who soon found it too weighty a burden and transferred it, a few days after, to the shoulders of Miramon, the most bitter "reactionist" of his party.

The Ministers of France, Spain and England appeared determined to recognize this bastard government, despite the fact that almost the whole country was in the hands of the liberals, and that almost every State adhered to the constitution of 1857. Mr. Otway, who represented Great Britain, had, while Miramon was General, demanded his dismissal for outrages committed upon British subjects at San Luis; but so soon as Miramon occupied the Presidential chair he formally recognized him. Miramon and Marquez soon after defeated the liberals at Tacubaya, entered the town, took seven "liberal" surgeons who were attending to the sick and wounded of both parties in the hospitals, and on April 11, 1859, shot them in cold blood. These were the acts of the party whom the allies were to shelter under their flag when a few years later the intervention was undertaken to prevent anarchy in Mexico and reinstate the conservative party, who, under Almonte, Miramon, Marquez, Zuloaga, Mejia, Miranda, and others, had spread devastation over their country.

The diplomatic corps had recognized Miramon the very day of his accession to power. Mr. Otway had passed directly through Vera Cruz, occupied by the legitimate government, to open relations with the last fire-brand which the church party was able to hold aloft at a moment when they only controlled the cities of Mexico and Puebla, with a few adjoining villages. So shamefully open was Mr. Otway's collusion with the clergy, that it caused his recall in July, 1859. He was superseded by Mr. Matthew. The church party appeared to possess peculiar and fascinating charms for the diplomatic representatives of foreign governments. Upon the arrival of Baron E. de Wagner, the representative of Prussia, they immediately won him to their support. M. Gabriac, the French minister, was so unscrupulous and powerful in support of the church that he was recalled and left on the 8th May, 1860.

In the meantime Zuloaga quarreled with Miramon, and demanded his restoration to power, maintaining that the Presidency had only been delegated to the latter as "President Substitute." Miramon refused to resign, and forced Zuloaga to accompany him on a campaign against the liberals. The diplomatic corps recognized the claims of Zuloaga, and on the 11th May they (with the exception of the Papal Nuncio and and the Minister of Guatemala) declared that there was no government existing in the capital. In August, upon the return of Miramon from his campaign, he called a junta of nineteen, was elected by them President of the Republic, and recognized as such by M. Pacheco, envoy from Spain. The reason of this recognition was obvious; it was to maintain intact the Mon-Almonte treaty which had been negotiated at Paris between Spain and the Miramon government in September, 1859, and which recognized claims previously ignored by every Mexican government. In a protest against this treaty, 30th January, 1860, the constitutional government called it "unjust in its essence, foreign to the usage of nations in the principles it established, illegal in the manner in which it was negotiated, and contrary to the rights of our country." This infamous treaty was afterwards to form a part of the Spanish claim against Mexico, at the time of the allied intervention.

The diplomatic corps were determined apparently to give the reactionists the longest possible lease of life. On the 21st October, 1860, the English Chargé withdrew to Jalapa and was soon followed by the Prussian Minister. In November the French Minister, M. Saligny, arrived, and proceeding immediately to Jalapa attempted to effect a compromise between the contending parties. Failing in this, he went to the capital, 20th December, 1862. The diplomatic corps now held a neutral position notwithstanding nearly the whole country was in the hands of the liberals. They were apparently awaiting the progress of events. It was at this time that their favorite, Miramon, broke into the British Legation and seized the "British bondholders' fund," after he had been completely beaten in a battle with the liberals, whose victorious troops entered the capital on the 25th December, 1860.

In a manifesto of the Constitutional Government, issued on the 20th January, 1861, upon its restoration to power, there is a spirit of reform, of progress, and the embodiment of modern civilization, which no liberal and civilized foreign government could ignore; for the stability of every modern power must depend upon the upholding and the propagation of such principles. This manifesto says: "The social reforms decreed at Vera Cruz, and which may be summed up in the nationalization of the property held in mortmain, freedom of religion and the consequent independence between the civil and spiritual power, are sanctioned by public opinion, have been the principal objects of the struggle, and in place of being in conflict with the constitution are only the development of the germ which it contains." "The government neither can nor could retrace its steps in the path of reforms which are so conformable to the spirit of the age, and that are the only means of reanimating and invigorating a society almost annihilated by inveterate abuses, and deep prejudices, and wasted by half a century of discord. The emancipation of the civil power, the liberty of conscience, and a respect for all beliefs, will assure peace, and will bring to the republic new elements of riches and of prosperity."

They determined to reorganize the judicial powers, to establish trial by jury, to have entire freedom of education, to establish primary and public schools, endow colleges and public institutes of science and progress, and grant complete liberty to the press.

Public improvements and the survey of the public lands were among the measures advocated. These and a fixed fiscal estimate were to restore the financial condition of the country to a sound condition, while proper taxation, protection to trade and foreign commerce, and the abolition of internal customs dues, were to aid in the general movement of progress and reform.

The army, instead of being swelled to such a proportion as to absorb all the revenues and endanger the stability of the government, was to be subordinate to the civil power, and limited to the actual necessities of the republic.

Almost breathless after a fierce struggle of fifty years, Mexico had at last brought these high principles to the surface of her stormy political sea.

Upon the success of the liberals, and the establishment throughout the whole country of the constitution of 1857, the people felt that they had at length freed themselves from the great curse which had borne so heavily upon them. It had taken fifty years, and there now seemed to open before them that long vista of prosperity for which the liberal statesmen had so long sighed, and for which they had every reasonable right to hope. All that was necessary for Mexico was to settle into the channel and follow the liberal principles which she had espoused. True, it was a herculean task which her patriots had to uphold. The chariot of Mars had so long rolled its wheels over the land that almost every element of stability, except the grasp of the clergy which still partially lingered, had been crushed out. Morality was almost a wreck; for it had been ground to powder between the ills of civil commotion and the corruption of the church. The finances of the government were not; and the liberals, poised upon the goal which their heroism had at last won, were forced to balance themselves by every means which might enable them to maintain their position until the resources of the country, trained in peaceful currents, might give them the means to restore their finances to a healthful condition. Their armor, torn, battered, and shattered in the greaves, through the sturdy blows which the church power had unceasingly rained upon it, needed repair; but scarcely had they taken breath before Europe was upon them, and again, with lance in rest for a tilt against the empire, they battle to restore the civilizing principles which they have unswervingly upheld, and which must finally triumph.

In the long series of revolutions through which Mexico has passed, the evil-minded of both parties—for that every cause has its traitors our late struggle with the South well proves—were not unmindful of their pockets. The governments, too, in order to maintain themselves, had negotiated loans at a ruinous discount, and sold valuable privileges existing in the country for almost a song. In 1841, General Bustamente effected a loan of $1,200,000. He received for it $200,000 cash, and one million in paper credits of the government, which were selling in the market for nine cents on the dollar. So hard pressed at one time was the government, that it sold the coining privilege of Guanajuato for fourteen years, receiving therefor $71,000 cash, when they were offered $400,000, if they would take it in yearly installments of $25,000 each. The "Reactionists" had stripped the country of almost every element of wealth upon which they could lay hands, regardless of consequences. They had maintained a perfect system of brigandage in every department; the onerous taxes which they had imposed being but the very lightest part of the burden to which the people were subjected. In September, 1860, M. Lefevre, a resident of Mexico at the time, relates that "General Miramon called together a new assembly of twenty-six capitalists, and demanded of them, according to his invariable custom, revolver in hand, the trifle of £100,000 sterling." Again, the "defenders of order" determined to seize £152,000 sterling belonging to British bondholders. This cash was in the safes of the British legation, and protected by the British seals. General Marquez, charged with the task, in a letter entirely unique, demanded that the funds "which might, under existing circumstances, run great risks in case of disturbance," should be delivered up for safe keeping to the Commissary General. The legation refused to deliver it; and the seals, bearing the arms of England, were broken, and the money removed by the church party. Marquez afterwards received the cordon of "Commander of the Legion of Honor," probably for committing a deed so essential to give the allied intervention a coloring of justice.

The liberal government, required by its position to gain time, until, by regenerating the country, they might restore health to the finances, was absolutely forced, through inability to comply with the treaties which the evil rule of the reactionists had foisted upon the country in an unfortunate hour, to decree the postponement of the payment of interest on all foreign debts for two years. So exhaustive had been the rule of their predecessors that there was absolutely nothing left with which to carry on the government from day to day. Of the revenues received upon French imports but eight per cent. were available for government use, while upon English imports all but twenty-five per cent. had been pledged for payments to foreign bondholders. The act of the suspension of the payment of interest on foreign debts, linked with the mountain of unredressed grievances of the previous years, enabled the French and British ministers to come to an open rupture with the government. In a correspondence with the latter the Mexican Secretary of State said: "So great, indeed, was their respect for these funds that they preferred to sacrifice their obligations to Mexicans, to trample under foot the most cherished principles of their country—nay, even to imprison persons of the highest respectability, in order to obtain resources from the sum paid for their release—rather than touch a cent of the assignments destined for the diplomatic convention and the London debt." Sir Charles Wyke, in his answer, said: "A starving man may justify in his own eyes the fact of his stealing a loaf on the ground that imperious necessity impelled him thereto." The retort of the Mexican Minister was apt: "It would be rather that of a father overwhelmed with debts, who, with only a small sum at his disposal, scarcely sufficient to maintain his children, employed it in the purchase of bread instead of the payment of his bills." The Mexican government was actually so poor at this time that it could not provide their minister to France enough money to pay his passage home.

It appeared that foreign governments, reasoning that nothing but anarchy—not great principles—had been established by the long and dismal period of revolutionary contests between liberal and almost obsolete ideas, were willing, at the very moment when the battle had been finished, the victory won, and a liberal, progressive government established over the land which had been so long priest-ridden, to press to the wall the liberalists, and throw a cloud over the rising sun of Mexican glory. The liberals, exhausted of treasure, with naught left them but their own good swords, and after a sanguinary and terrible struggle of fifty years for principles which every civilized nation has inscribed in its code of laws, now found themselves likely to be assailed by a wave from those very nations which pretended to teach them the science of government. It was destined to dash upon them, retard their progress and add its desolation to the land which Europe had already cursed.

Meanwhile the clergy were active with their machinations. Miramon was busy in Spain, where O'Donnell, the prime minister, lent a willing ear to the flattering hope that Mexico was now ready, like a ripe peach, to drop into the hands of any prince whom Spain might feel disposed, by the aid of a little force, to place upon the throne of her former viceroyalty. The hope was too much in common with the Spanish dream of restored colonial rule to be treated lightly, and an expedition was already upon the eve of organization for the benefit of the

Mexican clergy, for the redress of manifold grievances, and for the insult to her Minister, Señor Pacheco, who had been expelled from Mexico for meddling in the politics of the country.

PART V.

CAUSE OF THE ALLIANCE BETWEEN FRANCE AND ENGLAND—MOTIVES ALLEGED FOR THE INTERVENTION—OBJECTS OF SPAIN—PLANS OF ENGLAND—THE AUSTRIAN ELEMENT—THE TRUMPED-UP FINANCIAL CLAIMS—SIGNING OF THE TREATY OF ALLIANCE—SEIZURE OF VERA CRUZ BY SPAIN—DISCOURAGEMENT OF THE ALLIES—TREATY OF LA SOLEDAD—DEMANDS OF THE ALLIES—THEY QUARREL—ENGLAND AND SPAIN WITHDRAW THEIR FORCES—GROSS VIOLATION OF THE TREATY OF LA SOLEDAD BY FRANCE—THE CHURCH PARTY THROW OFF THE MASK—DEFEAT OF THE FRENCH AT PUEBLA—THE EFFECT IN FRANCE—ARRIVAL OF GENERAL FOREY—SIEGE AND FALL OF PUEBLA—THE APPOINTMENT OF NOTABLES—ILLEGAL ELECTION OF MAXIMILIAN TO BE EMPEROR—IT IS SANCTIONED BY A PRETENDED POPULAR VOTE—RUPTURE OF THE FRENCH WITH THE CHURCH PARTY WHO ISSUE A PROTEST—MISTAKES OF NAPOLEON III—THE PROMISED FRENCH EVACUATION—POSITION OF THE UNITED STATES ON THE MEXICAN QUESTION.

WE come now to the causes of the union of France and England in this expedition, whose inception was Spanish; and although it is a matter which will not admit of a clearly mathematical demonstration, owing to the lack of documents which are behind the scenes, we may hope at least to show why France deemed it to her interests to establish a throne in Mexico. In the instructions to General Forey, 3d of July, 1862, after the mask had been thrown off and France had been left alone in her pursuit of conquest, the Emperor Napoleon said: "In the present state of the civilization of the world the prosperity of America is not a matter of indifference to Europe, for it is that country which feeds our manufactories and gives an impulse to our commerce. We have an interest in the republic of the United States being powerful and prosperous, but not that she should take possession of the whole of the Gulf of Mexico, thence command the Antilles as well as South America, and be the only dispenser of the products of the New World." * *

"We now see how precarious is the lot of a branch of manufacture which is compelled to procure its raw material in a single market—all the vicissitudes of which it has to bear." * * "If, on the contrary, Mexico maintains her independence and the integrity of her territory; if a stable government be there constituted, with the assistance of France, we shall have restored to the Latin race on the other side of the Atlantic all its strength and its prestige; we shall have guaranteed security to our West India colonies, and to those of Spain; we shall have established our friendly influence in the center of America, and that influence, by creating immense markets for our commerce, will procure us the raw materials indispensable for our manufactures."
* * * "Mexico, thus regenerated, will always be well-disposed towards us, not only out of gratitude, but also because her interests will be in accord with ours, and because she will find support in her friendly relations with European Powers."

Here, then, were the true causes of the expedition which, condensed, meant the commercial and political aggrandizement of France, and the interposition of a barrier to the extension of the great Republic. There was, however, one more element all powerful with the French Emperor. It was the glory of the Catholic faith throughout Christendom, as the champion of which France now stands foremost. We cannot forget that Pepin, the son of Charles Martel, wanted the Crown of France, and that a contract was made between him and Pope Zachary, in 752, whereby Pepin became king, and the Pope was freed from Constantinople and the Lombards; that the next year Pope Stephen II. visited France, anointed Pepin with the "holy oil," in the monastery of St. Denis, and thus indissolubly linked the throne of France to the Vatican. The influence has never been lost, and France, by her power, has in latter years, become the exponent of the church militant in Europe; the mantle of Spain, as the "Bulwark of Christendom," falling upon her shoulders. In the restoration of the Catholic power in Mexico, to a healthy condition, we must find one of the most powerful of the causes of the French intervention, and the chair of St. Peter propped up, as it is to-day, by French bayonets, is not backward in demanding of its faithful adherents the regeneration of the Mexican church. To-day France has done in Mexico what M. Billault, in the Corps Legislatif, 7th February, 1864, said she had done in China: "We have penetrated into the heart of China to plant at the same time the symbol of our faith, which we protect, and to open a world to our commerce."

Another powerful reason for the French occupation of Mexico, is its commanding position, which is salient above all other countries, as we have shown in the opening of this paper. We may point to the fact that since the rule of the Emperor Napoleon III. the policy of France has been to extend in all direction her colonial interests, and in common with her great rival, England, whose policy she emulates, to gain possession, either by force or purchase, of all the prominent and controlling points of the globe. At the Isthmus of Suez, in the face of Engineering difficulties pronounced by English engineers insurmountable, French science cuts through from the Mediterranean to the Red Sea, and reconnecting the waters united by Rameses II. more than a score of centuries ago, reopens this old gate to the riches of the Indies, and adds one more glory to the greatness of France. It is the same with Mexico on the west as with Egypt on the east. France seeks the control of both these great commercial avenues. At the mouth of the Red Sea, another great point for the control of that East India route has fallen into her possession, while in the Corps Legislatif a French minister boasts "that between Singapore and China an immense and magnificent possession takes under our flag a rapid march towards a brilliant future."

The reasons which France gave for the Mexican intervention were the merest bubbles upon the great ocean of other interests which she saw for her future glory, providing her efforts were successful, as from the then condition of the great Republic she had every reason to believe they would be. M. Billault, in the speech quoted above, says of Mexico: "There, also, great political vistas are opened to clear-sighted eyes; diverse interests come in contact, and it is not opportune to neglect them."

Pressed powerfully by the emissaries of the clergy to make good their cause in Mexico against the liberals, and actuated by all the incentives to conquest which we have detailed, France was not dilatory in deciding to become an active participant in the enterprise. We shall see further on that she could not carry out her views in this unless Spain should concede to her the foremost position, not only as defender of the faith, but in respect to the commercial and colonial policy which so largely controlled the expedition.

The objects which Spain had were, in compliance with the wishes of the Mexican church, to establish the old system, and, if possible, to restore the lost jewels of the Spanish crown, by the creation of a monarchy in Mexico, with the enthronement of the Count of Flanders, younger brother of the heir of King Leopold of Belgium, who was to espouse a Spanish infanta, and thus, as a Madrid ministerial journal proclaimed in December,

1861 :—" If the throne of Mexico were not to be occupied by a Spanish prince, it would at least be pressed by a Spanish princess." M. Mon, in 1861, before the date of the allied treaty of intervention, wrote to the Spanish Ambassador at Paris :—" The government should not conceal that this may be a suitable occasion for awakening ancient recollections, and placing upon the throne of Mexico a prince of the blood of the Bourbons more or less intimately united to that house." Soon following this (September 10, 1861) came the Spanish invitation to the allies to join in the intervention. In the unhappy revolutionary condition of Spanish America, it has been the dream of Spain to restore her former viceroyal dependencies to her crown, or at least, as we see here, erect monarchies under the rule of Bourbon princes. Spain has never ceased to hug this delusion, and it gave rise to the war which for three years she lately waged unsuccessfully against San Domingo, under the idea that the erring child was ready to receive again the lash and rod which for centuries made her horrors a proverb. Spain seizes the Chincha Islands, Peru protests, some trouble occurs in the premises, and Spain demands $3,000,000 indemnity. Chile refuses to salute her flag and Spain declares war, only to show to mankind how weak the quicksilver of the New World has made her bones. She takes no lessons of the intellectual giant of La Mancha, and proves herself the great Don Quixote of the nineteenth century.

The plans of England were essentially commercial. She sought no conquest in the intervention ; the giant has grasped at last all the territory that his muscles can defend and now asks nothing but peace. The athlete has won his victories, established his reputation, and now, in possession of a long list of commercial outposts, and a line of island sentinels encircling and commanding the world, is quite contented to be peaceful, monopolize commerce and manufactures and grow fat—quite contented to send a ship or two to Mexico to see that the interest on the British bonds be paid, and that his commercial relations shall remain undisturbed. She had an interest also in preventing Spain from again gaining control over the Spanish Americas, whereby the immense commerce of England with them might be hampered, as it had been by Spanish policy when she held the power there and for two centuries baffled English attempts to gain a foothold. In the Spanish Cortes it was advocated that England joined solely "to prevent Spain from undertaking it alone." Great Britain was not unwilling either to plant a barrier, by establishing, through " moral support," a stable government in Mexico, which might curb the growth of her young offspring, the great Republic, who breakfasts on Louisiana, lunches on Florida and Texas, dines on New Mexico, Arizona, and the Pacific slope, and, it is feared, will sup upon Mexico. It is true that, as a matter of politeness, the United States were invited; but, as the allies agreed before the treaty of October 31, 1861, was signed, "Operations might be commenced without awaiting the answer of the American government."

The policy of France, as was well known and canvassed in Paris before the sailing of the expedition, was the placing of the Austrian Archduke Maximilian upon the throne of Mexico, through the "moral support" of the army. During the month of the signing of the treaty of intervention, the French Minister of Foreign Affairs, speaking of the dissolution of Mexico, said:—"Such an event cannot be a matter of indifference to England; and the principal means, in our opinion, to prevent its accomplishment, would be the establishment in Mexico of a regenerative government strong enough to arrest its internal dissolution." Then, speaking of the disinterestedness of France, he says: "Desirous of respecting the susceptibilities of all parties, it would see with pleasure the choice of the Mexicans fall upon a prince of the house of Austria." M. Thouvenel wrote, October 15, 1861, to M. Barrot, French Ambassador at Madrid, that, in case of an eventual return of a monarchy in México: —"The Emperor, foreseeing such an eventuality, with perfect disinterestedness resigned beforehand all candidature for any prince of the imperial family; and he did not doubt that the other two governments entertained similar dispositions. Finally, that in regard to the choice of a dynasty, in the eventuality indicated, we had no candidate to propose, but that should the fact happen, an Austrian prince would meet with our assent." We shall see later how Spain, forced gradually into a secondary position, instead of holding to her primary one, yielded to her great rival and embarked her forces for home. It is a settled fact that France formed her plans for the establishment of a monarchy before the expedition was organized, and she fixed upon the Archduke as the one whom she would place upon the Mexican throne.

The allies being agreed, it was necessary on the part of France to find some good pretext for intervention. The best one upon which she could fix was the debts due to her from Mexico. But notice the smallness of these. In 1863 M. Jules Favre stated before the legislative Assembly that "Mexico was our debtor, according to treaty signed, for $750,000. There were other claims, but they were conditional. The amount did not reach 5,000,000 francs" ($1,000,000). There was also the Jecker debt of $15,000,000, which France held in reserve for her ultimatum. We shall speak hereafter of the Jecker claim, which was one of the most scandalous frauds ever perpetrated. A large number of fraudulent Mexican and Spanish claims were procured insertion into the "English convention," for which Great Britain now urged a settlement. This diplomatic convention was for $5,000,000, of which but $266,000 belonged to English subjects.

Added to all the reasons which Western Europe had for the intervention, the clergy had brought all their spiritual and temporal ordnance to bear to effect it. They left no power unemployed; even their old champion, Santa Anna, from his place of exile, St. Thomas, still exerted his influence to the utmost to seat a King upon the throne which the shade of the Montezumas has cursed for any occupant. He wrote, October 15, 1861, to Estrada: "What you have to do is to remind the governments near which you are accredited of your former petitions, insisting especially that Mexico cannot have a lasting peace until the disease is radically cured, and the only remedy is the substitution of a constitutional empire for that farce called a republic. Those nations can select one jointly. Remind them also that I am now more than ever disposed to carry out that idea, and that I will labor without ceasing to effect it." Still true to his party, the church, he hoped also to effect great benefits "by restoring the Catholic religion."

The pragmatic treaty between the allies was at length signed at London, October 31, 1861. Its stipulations were peculiar, and showed the jealousy with which the parties watched each other. The second article stated that "the high contracting parties engage not to seek for themselves, in the employment of the coercive measures contemplated by the present convention, any acquisition of territory or any special advantage, and not to exercise in the internal affairs of Mexico any influence of a nature to prejudice the right of the Mexican nation to choose and to constitute freely the form of its government." How well Napoleon III. kept this treaty, to which he solemnly swore, the sequel proves.

The Power which could take the initiative in the movement, and which sent the largest force, was naturally the one to direct the future policy of the country which Spain and France went to conquer. Both of these Powers made undue haste to reach the scene of their labors; so great, indeed, that they neglected almost everything that could tend to the success of the expedition. The allies were to rendezvous at Cuba; but the Spanish contingent sailed before the French and English arrived, seized upon the Mexican port of Vera Cruz, and on December 14, 1861, the Spanish commander issued a proclamation to the people of Mexico. It had been quick work, for the treaty of of London had been signed only forty-four days before, and Spain had thus gained a move on France. The allies soon after arrived; the whole expedition numbered in soldiers, sailors and marines, about 19,000. Of these the English furnished only about 700 marines, France about 2,500 effective soldiers, and Spain about 6,000, the balance being sailors. It is a notable fact, that the nation whose grievances were greatest, and which had the largest money debt due from Mexico, furnished absolutely no regular forces for the purpose of invasion. It proves that Article II., which we have quoted from the treaty of London, was inserted entirely at the dictation of England, and that she entered the expedition with the intention, so far as lay in her power, to prevent either of her allies from stealing a march upon her and affecting her future in the New World.

The allies had landed without war equipments suitable to the campaign which they were about to undertake; they were unprovided with camp equipage or means of transportation. The emissaries of the clergy had represented to them that the whole country was ready to throw itself into their arms and accept any government which they might dictate; but the monarchical party who were to effect a revolution did nothing; on the contrary, every day the liberal government grew stronger. Admiral Jurien de la Gravière, seeing the falsity of the representations of the "reactionists" which had been presented to France, wrote to General Prim, in command of the Spanish forces, saying: "I have always been disposed to agree with you in recognizing the necessity we are under here to avoid embracing the cause of the party which composes the minority and which has opposed to it the general opinion of the country." France had counted upon obtaining supplies and mules from the inhabitants, but found that they would not sell them at any price. General Uraga, commanding the liberal forces, laid waste the country around them, and they found almost the whole Mexican people ready to receive them at the point of the bayonet.

The allies were thus subjected to great straits for provisions, which, linked to the sickness of the coast and the rapidly approaching season of the "vomito," made their cause look most dismal. The Spanish force had already two thousand sick in hospital, the English one hundred and thirty sick out of seven hundred, and the French were in much the same condition. They then requested from the very government which they came to overthrow, the privilege of encamping their troops upon the high ground inland, where, free from the miasma of the *tierra caliente*, they might open negotiations with a govern-

ment whose existence they had ignored before their departure from Europe. It was a humility before the world which they had not anticipated. They had traversed six thousand miles of water to find that Mexico had a government; and that she required no other form to preserve peace and maintain the laws of the land. They had in Europe proclaimed that the government of Juarez was without faith, without honor; that no treaty could be made with it without guarantees; that it was a perfect farce to treat under any circumstances with such perjurers; and yet, the very first article of the "Treaty of La Soledad," which, after the allied ultimatum had been sent forward, was the opening of negotiations, and which received the signatures of the representatives of the allied Powers, was:—
First, "Admitting that the constitutional government, which at present directs the affairs of Mexico, has manifested to the commissioners of the allied Powers that it has no need whatever of the assistance so kindly offered to the Mexican people, as having at its own disposal sufficient elements of force and public opinion to maintain itself against all intestine revolt, the allies, therefore, deem it their duty to enter upon the way of treaties for the purpose of drawing up the claims which they have to make in the name of their respective nations."

In article second the allies protest "that they will attempt nothing against the independence, sovereignty and integrity of the territory of the republic." Here the allies, then, plainly admit that Mexico is perfectly able to manage her own affairs. This treaty had arisen from the necessity of an ultimatum to the Mexican government which should embody the demands of the allies; but it was a matter of no small difficulty for the commissioners to agree upon the amounts to be demanded. It was claimed on the part of France that each power had a right to fix its own reclamations, regardless of the others. The truth is that France and Spain had, in their attempts to overreach each other, taken no time to consider the amounts justly their due. France, taking care to have her demands cover all contingencies, fixed her ultimatum at twelve million dollars. The immediate execution of the Jecker contract, which had been made with the government of Miramon when tottering to its fall, was also required. Jecker was a Swiss banker who, after passing through twenty years of the vicissitudes of Mexican commercial life, during which time he was engaged in many doubtful enterprises, at length entered into a contract with the government of Miramon to negotiate a loan of $15,000,000, out of which, by several very doubtful financiering moves, he reaped $14,250,000 in bonds, and Miramon and his church party $750,000 cash.

The demands of the allies amounted, without the Jecker claim, to $40,000,000, or four times the yearly revenue of Mexico. The parties were surprised at each other's claims; especially did the Spanish and English commissioners demur at the pressing of the Jecker fraud into the demand, which would swell it to $55,000,000, a sum which they knew it was impossible for Mexico immediately to pay. They finally were so uncertain what to require, that they sent forward the ultimatum, which was so very vague in its demands that the astute statesmen of Mexico saw in it the germs of the confusion which was to take place in the councils of their invaders, and acted accordingly. Their object was to gain time, which was admirably accomplished in one of the articles of the "Treaty of La Soledad" above mentioned. All negotiations were there postponed until the 15th of April, 1862.

When the news reached France of the capture of Vera Cruz by the Spaniards, and the march which they had stolen on the Emperor Napoleon III., a reinforcement of four thousand five hundred men was immediately dispatched to Mexico, under command of General Lorencez, a brave and able officer, who was, upon his arrival, to assume command of the whole French contingent. General Prim, upon the unexpected appearance of the French reinforcements, saw Spain forced into the secondary position, which crushed all the finely prepared theories with which Spain had deluded herself. He therefore at once began to oppose objections to the claims which France demanded of Mexico, being especially loud in his protests against the infamous Jecker claim, to which the minister from England was also bitterly opposed. Another very serious cause of complaint, and which, under the circumstances, was magnified into a pretence for the withdrawal of Spain and England from the coalition, was the presence in the French camp of Almonte, the "infamous Marquez," and others of the monarchical or "reactionary" party, who had, although outlawed, entered Mexican territory under protection of the French flag, and commenced issuing "pronunciamientos" and inflammatory appeals to the people after the usual style of inciting a Mexican revolution. Miramon had also landed at Vera Cruz, but the English threatened to arrest him for his wholesale robbery of their Legation, before mentioned, and he was obliged to flee to Havana.

The constitutional government demanded that the traitors and outlaws under protection of the French flag should be given up or leave the country; but the French commander refused so just a demand. He was little inclined to give up the leaders of the church party, whose cause his master, the French

Emperor, had espoused. General Prim and Sir Charles Wyke considered that these demands were perfectly just, and insisted that President Juarez had a right to consider the retention of these outlaws as a declaration of war against the government. M. de Saligny protested that General Almonte had the confidence of the French government, and that he could not be expelled from their camp. The controversy grew warm; linked with the exorbitant exactions of France in the ultimatum, the Spanish and English commissioners, foreseeing the result which proved them to have been duped from the origin of the expedition, retired to Vera Cruz and embarked their troops for Europe in April, 1862. France was thus left to play out the game, in whose primary moves she had been so successful, in accordance with the course which had been fixed upon from the inception of the enterprise.

The fourth article of the "Treaty of La Soledad" stipulated that, "in order that it may not in the most remote degree be believed that the allies have signed these preliminaries in order to obtain the passage of the fortified positions garrisoned by the Mexican army, it is stipulated that, in the unfortunate event of the negotiations being broken off, the forces of the allies will retire from the said towns, and will place themselves in the line that is beyond the said fortifications on the Vera Cruz side; Paso Ancho on the Cordova road, and Paso de Ovejas on that of Jalapa, being the principal extreme points."

In gross violation of the treaty, the French refused to comply with this article, under plea that the sick in hospital would be forced to remain in Orizaba, and there be exposed to danger. Totally ignoring all honorable action, they retained possession of this powerful stronghold which it might have cost them thousands of their best troops to capture, if we may judge from the opposition they afterwards encountered in their march towards the capital. The unhealthiness of the Vera Cruz district, in which, had they returned, their forces might have been almost annihilated, was another reason which no doubt caused them to break faith with the Mexicans. The plea which they urged was the merest subterfuge. Even General Prim pressed them to fall back beyond the first lines of fortifications which they had passed under solemn treaty, and through the generosity which the Mexican government evinced in behalf of the sanitary condition of the invading force. He assured them that the sick would be as well cared for by the Mexicans as they would be at any hospital in Paris. All effort was, however, useless; inveighing as the French did against Mexican perfidy, their first act upon the soil was as perfidious as any they came to avenge.

The church party, in the French camp, now threw off the mask. Almonte immediately issued a *pronunciamiento* to the Mexicans, proclaiming himself Chief of the nation, and gathered under his standard a few of the predatory bands which, under the fostering care of the clergy, had never ceased to deluge the country in blood. Almonte issued paper money, dictated his dispatches, created and dismissed generals, and maintained, under French protection, the complete semblance of a government in full operation. The French thus commenced to "pacify the country."

General Lorencez, who had replaced Admiral Jurien in command of the French forces, now advanced towards Mexico to afford that "moral support" to the Mexicans which they so much desired. He anticipated, through the representations of the church party, that he had only to march inland to be welcomed as the savior and liberator of the country; that the people who in one year, 1858, had fought in civil warfare seventy-one engagements, out of which eight were pitched battles, would rise *en masse* to welcome a foreign invading force, and that the phantom of a constitutional government under Juarez would vanish before him. Surely the French Emperor cannot be so poor a judge of human nature, or imagine there exists so vile a people on the face of this earth that they will not defend themselves under any circumstances from foreign invasion; and yet how closely France has hugged this delusion for several years past may be seen by the thousands of French troops she has buried under the soil of Mexico, and the millions of treasure she has wasted in the pursuit of an idea which it is hardly her destiny to realize.

We need not detail the defeat which the brave General Lorencez received at Puebla on the 5th May, 1862, the heroic fortitude with which he sustained his little army in the intrenchments of Orizaba after his retreat from Puebla, and during the interval in which he was obliged to await reinforcements from France. The French did all that brave soldiers and a good general could do with such a force against Mexico united instead of divided.

The news of the defeat of Lorencez and the terrible slaughter of the French troops before Puebla was a shock which France was but poorly prepared to receive. It was suddenly discovered that the French troops had something more than a promenade to make in Mexico. French honor now came in as one of the primary elements of the problem. General Forey was dispatched with large reinforcements, and with orders to assume entire command, both political and military, of the expedition.

Upon the arrival of General Forey at Orizaba, with the

reinforcements, he also discovered that he would be long detained at that point before he could place his forces in such marching order as might be required for the "pacification of the country." He issued a proclamation from Orizaba to the Mexican people. Said he: "In the name of the Emperor I declared to you solemnly what I again repeat to you to-day—namely, that the soldiers of France have not come here to impose upon you a government." * * * "That they have no other mission but that of consulting the national wish as to the form of government it may desire." What would France exclaim to-day if, against her united people, the nations of Europe were to march upon Paris with such a manifesto? Now, either General Forey was deceiving the Mexican people or disobeying his orders, for the Emperor, in his famous letter of instructions in July, 1862, wrote: "The demands of our policy, the interest of our industry and our commerce all impose upon us the duty of marching upon Mexico, there boldly planting our flag and establishing perhaps a monarchy, if not incompatible with the national sentiment of the country, but at least a government that will promise some stability." Compare these instructions with the following extract from a letter of the Emperor to Géneral Lorencez, in 1862: "It is contrary to my interest, my origin and my principles to impose any kind of government whatever on the Mexican people. They may freely choose that which suits them best."

Almost a year after the defeat of Lorencez the French forces under Marshal Forey again sat down before Puebla, and with forty thousand men, assisted by the renegades and bandits who, under Almonte and Marquez, added their strength to the French troops, commenced a siege which was to take rank in heroic defence with Numantia, Saguntium and Saragoza. General Ortega commanded the city, assisted by able generals and able engineers, such as Generals Paz, Colombres and others, to whom very much of the credit of the defence belongs. Inch by inch the desperate defenders of the city contended with the assailants; barricade after barricade sprung up before the French, and every foot of ground gained was at the cost of a score of brave men; whole blocks of buildings, with their defenders, were undermined and blown into the air. It was only after the most desperate onslaught that the assailants could make any impression upon the works. For two months the French rained an unceasing fire upon the devoted city and its convents, which had been turned into forts; for two months the Mexicans gave their foes that "warm welcome" which they had been promised by the clergy before they left France. The city at length succumbed to the indomitable valor of the "pacificators," and

Marshal Forey soon after appeared before the capital, and entering it, took possession June 10, 1863.

In possession of the city, Marshal Forey immediately took measures to allow the Mexicans to select the form of government that pleased them. He appointed thirty-five notables, twenty-two of whom were former members of the reactionary government, and most of them of the junta of Miramon in 1863; all of them, however, of the church party. The notables immediately elected a regency of three, called the "Supreme Executive Power," designated to them by General Forey as men who would meet his views. These were General Almonte, General Salas, and the Archbishop of Mexico; they in turn elected a new assembly of notables, two hundred and fifteen in number.

The programme being all arranged, the Regency met on the 7th July. The principal mountebanks and jugglers being all in their places, up went the curtain and the farce of Maximilian I., or the moral pacification of Mexico was displayed before the world. The Regency named the notables, and then chose the form of government, which was to be an empire. With wonderful unanimity they elected the Archduke Maximilian to the throne. The notables, all good representatives of the reactionary party, confirmed the election, and, in a proclamation to the Mexican people, stated their reasons for this proceeding: "For forty years," said they, "Mexico has been governed by brigands, vagabonds and incendiaries." They had a wonderful loss of memory at that moment, for they forgot that for nearly the whole period it had been their party which had ruled, and that some of the very members who authorized this proclamation had committed some of the most glaring outrages which have blackened Mexican annals.

Thus the empire, after a terrible struggle, had birth by the Cæsarian process, and the next act was to offer to Maximilian the crown which the pacified Mexican people so willingly conferred. For this purpose a commission was dispatched to Austria; but the farce of allowing the Mexican people to select their own form of government had been so boldly and yet so stupidly enacted that, in the face of the public opinion of the world, Maximilian could not accept the crown thus offered to him, unless, to smooth over this most glaring outrage of the nineteenth century, a vote—a popular vote—might be taken, whereby it might be demonstrated to the nations that Mexico was indeed pacified; that it had welcomed its invaders; that there had in fact been no siege of Puebla, no bloody defeats and equally bloody victories; that all the heroes who fought under the constitutional banner of Juarez were bandits and outlaws, and all Christians, such as Miramon, Almonte, Marquez, Miranda, Mejia, and other "conservatives," who had for fifty years caused the country to reel in an intoxication of blood, were the only people who were tinctured with civilization, and who were indeed the lords of the soil; all who, with "liberty and reform" on their banners, and who would not vote for the new *régime*, being outcasts, unworthy of consideration, except through the constant and arduous employ of from forty to fifty thousand French troops to keep them from overturning the peaceable and unoffending clergy who represented the cause of "law and order."

Maximilian said to the commissioners, on the 3d of October, 1863, "My acceptance of the offered throne must therefore depend upon the result of the vote of the whole country." But the only way to obtain this vote was to make every Mexican citizen deposit his suffrage under the gleam of a French bayonet. It was reliably calculated by M. Malaspine, editor of "L'Opinion Nationale," that when General Bazaine was instructed in August to take the vote, seven-eighths of the population of Mexico and twenty-nine thirtieths of its territory were beyond the lines of French protection, while the territory which they occupied was overrun by seventy-two hostile guerilla bands, averaging from seventy to three hundred men each. General Bazaine thus found it necessary to organize his forces into separate divisions, and make what has wittily been called "an electioneering tour in favor of Prince Maximilian." The election was held, the dullest brain may imagine how. The country gave its popular vote for the Austrian archduke, who soon after satisfied with the result, ascended the throne of pacified Mexico. Thus the cause for which the Mexican people had for a half century battled and bravely won was thrown back years into the past. The Mexican Congress protested against the glaring outrage which foisted upon them a monarchical government through the aid of fifty thousand bayonets.

France had at length reached a point where it was necessary to adopt a policy of government suitable to the country and its future development; they analyzed and found the principles of the party whose cause they had espoused totally incompatible with the wants of Mexico, and in conformity with their consistency of action throughout the invasion, they now espoused the principles of the very party which had been so boldly battling to hold their country intact. General Bazaine came to an open rupture with the church party, which had betrayed the country into the hands of France. Their schemes, their guilty hopes, had borne their legitimate fruits; the clergy had expected that progress would be turned back upon itself, and that the old sys-

tem would be established, whereby the church might usurp all power, all wealth, and all emoluments. The French commander, with a keen insight into the troubles which environed the position, was forced, by maintaining the policy of the liberals, who had sequestrated the church property, to refuse its restoration to the clergy. Thus the invaders came to an open rupture with the bishops, and virtually acknowledged the justness of the cause for which the constitutionalists were battling. The archbishop of Mexico was removed from the regency to which Marshal Forey had appointed him. After some correspondence between the archbishop and General Bazaine, the prelates of Mexico issued a joint protest, which is in every view a remarkable document. Opening with a reproach to the French for having betrayed their holy Catholic faith, which the Emperor Napoleon III. had promised them should be restored in all its former rights and privileges, they protest at the treatment it has received, and state that it suffers "a compulsion in its most holy rights and in its canonical liberties entirely equal to that which it suffered when the authorities emanating from the Plan of Ayutla (the liberals) were in power." "Then," said they, "the government frankly manifested its principles; it appeared to the view of this Catholic people in the character of an opposition armed with a power against religion and the church; and the latter, as a victim immolated by the government, defended itself heroically, suffering the consequences of a terrible persecution, and perishing nobly for the holy cause of justice. * * * Then the prelates leaving our country, carried with them the hope that the first political change which should take place would bring with it a complete moral and religious restoration. To-day, returning after such a change, to be present at the immolation of all our principles, the consummation of the ruin of the church, we have received a blow such as is only received at the death of all human hope. Then the church had only one enemy—the government that persecuted it. To-day it has two—that same government which still lives in the country, which still has resources of its own; an army that contends hand to hand for every foot of ground, and that counts upon the aid of its principles and interests in the enemy's camp, and in the capital; an enemy whose first occupation it is to carry into effect the destructive plans of its opponents, in religious and moral affairs. * * *
Then we received a blow from the hands of an open enemy; to-day we are attacked by those who call themselves friends of the church and protectors of its liberties. * * *
Then we could publish our protests and our pastorals; to-day the press is bound in such a manner that it is only open to those

who favor the intervention." The whole document is a wail of woe at the betrayal of their hopes by those into whose hands they had betrayed their country. Seldom in history can we find a document so replete with the exasperation of disappointment. They acknowledge, too, finally, that the wars waged by the liberals are only against the opposition of the church to "liberty and reform." The clergy had thrown their bone before the lions of Europe, and now they were doomed to see it despoiled of its meat as strip after strip it was wrenched off. They had invited the invader to oppose the constitutional reforms of the liberals, only to see them, when firmly in power, espouse those reforms. It was a case of the most glaring inconsistency on all sides. France had proclaimed that she espoused the cause of the "reactionists;" she no sooner reached the capital than she overturned the cause she had espoused, and espoused the cause she had overturned, while at the same moment, with 50,000 troops, she battled against the brave defenders of these very principles which she now inscribed upon the code of Mexico. It was a bold proof that it was might not right which dictated the invasion, and that the ruler of France and his advisers were either in a most lamentable state of ignorance in reference to the history and political condition of the country, or else they warred for an idea, and chose to waste some of the best blood of France upon a soil which could yield them no return for the prodigal outlay, either in honor, justice, glory or wealth, but which might fix an indelible stain upon that glorious escutcheon which is almost as much the pride of the United States as of France.

On the 18th October, 1864, the Roman Pontiff addressed a letter to Maximilian, urging him to agree with the Mexican clergy; but Maximilian, in his instructions to his Minister of Justice, December 27th, 1864, totally disregards it, proposing on the contrary to declare religious tolerance, and confirm the reform laws of Juarez. This was followed on the 26th February, 1865, by a decree confirming these instructions; the protests of the clergy being useless. These measures had the effect upon the Mexican mind to bind them more firmly to the constitution of 1857, and to support the liberals upholding it, who were thus by their very invaders adjudged to be fighting for the right.

But Maximilian is enthroned, and we find it is necessary for France to retain 50,000 troops to sustain him where the suffrages of the people have placed him. It has now become a matter of pride to the French ruler to at least, if he cannot consolidate the monarchy which his "moral pacification" scheme has erected, to continue the farce with the hope that some lucky turn of fortune may enable him to reap the honors of a drawn game, where the liberals play as well with their knights and pawns as Napoleon with his king and bishops.

Napoleon III. made a great mistake in the character of the people whose territory he invaded. He should have taken a lesson from Napoleon I., whose genius was not sufficient to impose upon Spain a government with King Joseph at its head. The invasion of Spain by the great Napoleon at the opening of this century, was wonderfully similar in all its phases to the invasion of Mexico by his nephew in 1862; the same appointment of notables, and the same farce of imposing a foreign prince upon the people. The period of occupation of the countries will doubtless correspond very nearly. Said Talleyrand to the great Emperor, "Your Majesty will never hear the last shot fired in a war with a people who have fought eight hundred years with the Moors." Mexico, from the hearts of the liberals, echoes the same sentiment in reference to its own soil. The French monarch has forgotten that when France invaded the Peninsula Spain had but eleven million inhabitants, that she was in immediate contact with France, which might easily supply her invading forces with means to prosecute the war, or to rapidly reinforce any threatened point, and that, notwithstanding she poured some of her largest veteran armies into Spain, she could not conquer her. If France thus failed to conquer a kingdom lying at her very door, how could she hope to subdue a republic six thousand miles distant, with a territory nearly four and one-half times as large, and which contains eight millions of people, united in a common cause against her, and possessing a country eminently adapted to the partisan style of warfare which so harassed and cut up the troops of France in the Peninsula? In topographical features which might enable partisan bands to maintain a destructive warfare, Mexico is eminently like Spain. Her mountain ridges, her waterless deserts, her fastnesses, her numerous large towns and centers of population—which cannot all be held at once by an invading force—render her capable of a brilliant defence—and capable, too, to work out her own salvation against any number of troops which Napoleon may be able to bring against her in the present political condition of Europe.

We believe that all that France ever planned in reference to the future development of Mexico will be realized, but not through the influence of any invading Power; for, to hold and direct the energies of Mexico in a monarchical channel, you must change the political condition of the United States, and also its form of government. It would take a standing army of one hundred thousand foreign troops in Mexico to crush out the leaven of dissensions which would constantly impregnate the people from contact with us; and, as we are ceaselessly advancing westward with our civilization, and building up powerful States in our march, the effort to establish upon our frontiers a monarchy, under the shadow of any European flag, must, by the very abrasion of progressive ideas, fall in its own tracks, which denote a backward instead of an advancing pace in the order of the world's march westward.

We believe that there is a great law regulating the progress of the human race, and that, like the spheres which whirl round it, it has its orbit of revolution. May not its constant march westward gather to its folds an ever increasing civilization, as its resistless activity develops and calls forth a steady growth of brain force? Does not this advance of the human element, forcing before it the great wave of intellectual improvement, indicate that in future ages, when in its course it has swept across the Pacific and impinged upon the eastern Asiatic border, that the worn-out nationalities there found must move westward towards Europe—westward, westward, until, in the ceaseless revolution, they meet our American nationalities—then as dead as Asia is to-day—and, with a civilization and improvement which will have gained immensely in its revolution of the world, force us in our turn before its irresistible onward march? The effects of such invasions as that of France in Mexico may impede, but scarcely exert a perceptible influence upon the course of the race.

In the French expedition the French Emperor has played one of those far-reaching games so characteristic of him. A man who could reach the throne of France as he did must be blessed with a wonderfully good fortune, backed by a brain that has a deep insight into the fortuitous phases of any problem which may interest him; but in this Mexican problem he made a very excusable mistake, which altered its conditions entirely; this was, the predetermined result which, in common with Europe, he affixed to our civil war. It was, from the very outbreak of the rebellion, accepted as a foregone conclusion that the United States were divided never more to be united. Reasoning from all precedent, they had every right to draw this conclusion. It was supposed that the South, following the tendency of the institutions which existed there in 1860, would naturally gather the dominant classes into a powerful aristocratic faction, which, in consonance with their education and natural tendencies, would form a limited monarchical government. It could not have been entirely outside of the vista of Napoleon III. that in such an event the South might have found it to her advantage to link herself to Maximilian, and form with Mexico a great empire, of which the latter country would have been a dependency. France could then have more than enjoyed the reality of one of her dreams in reference to her Mexican conquest—not only the obtaining of cotton for herself, but almost its entire monopoly. It was also a very wise plan during our great contest to be within easy reach at the bursting of the Western stars. There were mighty and valuable fragments to be gathered up in such an event. They could not see the result through the convex achromatic lenses of liberty, in the nineteenth century; but chose rather to look at the movement through the concave goggles which monarchical Europe puts on whenever she looks at anything republican in the Old or New World.

It is worthy of consideration that, in April, 1861, the first gun thundered against Fort Sumter; in June the French legation pushed the liberal Mexican government to the wall; in October the allied treaty of intervention was signed; and, in the December following, Vera Cruz was occupied by a part of the allied force.

We are officially informed that the French troops will all be removed from the Mexican soil by November, 1867; "the first being intended to depart in November, 1866." There is an immensity between intention and action. We do believe that the French troops will be withdrawn, providing there are no further troubles in the United States before the time fixed; for the French people are thoroughly disgusted with this Mexican expedition, which draws so heavily both upon their pockets and their honor. There are, however, elements in the problem which place the Emperor Napoleon in a most embarrassing position—the honor of France and the prestige of his constant successes, which, if here broken, will cut loose the ties which have bound his name with so much firmness to that country. The French people have long been dazzled with the bright sun of the house of Bonaparte; once let them clear their eyes of this blindness, and there is little doubt what direction the erratic and highly organized brain of France would take. Heaven was in a prodigal mood when it shaped French intellect; and if in 1789 it surged in one wild wave beyond the level which liberty should occupy, it did no more than other nations have done before it; the reflux naturally brought back monarchy, but the tide vibrates still in its course to a proper equilibrium.

The withdrawal of the French troops does not necessarily involve the withdrawal of the French population in Mexico. The French troops, if naturalized there, may become Mexican troops under the banner of Maximilian. The time also of many of the French regiments may expire before November, 1867, and it is not a matter of compulsion that they should return home. Any foreigner may in Mexico to-day, or next year, enlist under the Mexican flag of Maximilian; and although he might have an army of thirty to forty thousand Frenchmen in his service, there might not be a single one of its soldiers borne upon the military roll of France. We believe, therefore, that whatever troops are withdrawn will be very few, and only those who cannot be persuaded to remain in the service of Maximilian. This is something to which we could not take exception, for France could justly say she no longer held a direct interest in the expedition, however large a quantity of funds she might furnish to support the bogus monarchy against the stalwart blows of the heroic liberals.

France labors under another difficulty : there is no reasonable course which she can pursue to obtain indemnity for the immense outlays which she has made in this expedition. She has, as it were, with an invading army, proclaimed Maximilian Emperor of Mexico; but he, never having been in possession of a square foot of ground which French troops have not for the moment occupied, has been unable to exercise his so-called function unless guarded by the bayonets which not only protect, but think and dictate his policy, making him the most perfect android of this century. What right has he to acknowledge a debt of 270,000,000 francs on the part of Mexico to France, or yet to negotiate a Mexican loan, as has been done on the French Bourse ? Being a mere puppet in the hands of the military power, he is, as it were, an officer of the invading force, who, within a mobilized encampment, with guns shotted and troops ready to spring to arms at the sound of the "long roll," signs a treaty and binds the country he invades to a course of action which the real government cannot, for a moment, sanction. Deny the existence of the liberal government all they may, the fact that fifty thousand French troops, with all their splendid discipline, war material, and equipment, cannot, or do not, to-day, hold one-third of the country against the half-starved and poorly supplied patriots opposed to them, is the most tangible and powerful recognition that can be granted that there is a force superior to their own, which, if the French Foreign Minister does not recognize, the Treasury of France does, and that, too, every day, with immense and constantly increasing additions to the debit side of the account, while the credit side is as blank as the soul which gave the expedition birth. The truth is, France sends an expedition to Mexico, sets up her android upon what she classifies as a throne, writes out her bill of indemnity, orders it to be signed, and lo! Mexico owes France at least $200,000,000.

If France evacuates Mexico and Maximilian follows, with whom can Napoleon treat? The allies acknowledged the existence of the liberal government by the treaty of La Soledad, when they first entered the country; and, as we have said, fifty thousand troops have recognized it ever since; but if, by a treaty on any subject, they again recognize that government they have so constantly ignored, it will be a virtual acknowledgment that they have never, in truth, been able to foist upon the country their bogus monarchy, and therefore its acts must fall with it, including the debts which have been contracted in the attempt to maintain it upon such unpromising soil. In truth the constitutional government has ever been since the French invasion the real government, and never has there been at any moment one-third of the country under the shadow of foreign bayonets.

The Emperor Napoleon is unfortunately bound, to a certain degree, to protect the prince of Austria, who was induced to place himself in so doubtful a position; the honor of France is here also at stake. In a discussion in the French Chambers, in January, 1864, M. Thiers boldly stated, that "when a prince is taken from one of the greatest reigning families of Europe, when that family is asked for a prince to be delivered up to the hazards of those civil wars so frequent in Mexico, to pretend that there is no obligation contracted towards him and his, is to advance a theory not very honorable to France." France, then, is assailed by a double dishonor. If she withdraws from Mexico and abandons Maximilian to his fate, she acknowledges her Mexican expedition a complete failure, and sinks much glory, much treasure, and much prestige on this side of the Atlantic, while, on the other side, it is equivalent to almost open war with Austria. French treasure and Austrian troops naturally become the next expedient. When that policy fails, will not a European war be necessary to give employment to the French mind and gloss over the Mexican failure? It is far from improbable that the reaction of the French Mexican scheme may cause Europe some trouble, and may lead to complications not to be measured by words, but by swords.

In our present condition in the United States, the result of four years of civil strife and terrible carnage, we are naturally left in a position where the elements are still simmering under the latent heat which produced the great rebellion. Aside from our abstract views of foreign interference in the governments of our Western World, we have a home interest to look to, which is not among the least important. All unsettled as we are, and seeking, as yet, to mingle the States into a more homogeneous nationality, the presence of a foreign monarchical element upon our southwestern frontier is a constant source, if not of alarm, at least of suspicion, which calls our earnest attention to its removal at the earliest moment. We do not want a war with France; we are too closely bound in the ties which were woven in our War of Independence to wish to live in other than the most amicable relations with her; but it is the feeling of the whole nation that this French-Mexican scheme is a constant threat against our people, which, if long continued, can but ripen into bitter fruit and destroy a friendship which we highly prize so long as we can enjoy it with honor. We feel that the time set for the withdrawal of the French forces is too distant, and that it is fixed more with reference to the hope that some lucky turn of events in the United States may leave the Mexican expedition undisturbed, than it is with a view to an abandonment of the Mexican scheme of empire. We hazard little in predicting that the Mexican question has scarcely yet reached its secondary phase.

Notwithstanding our warning to Austria not to embark troops to replace those of France in Mexico, reliable news reaches us that the first shipment of such troops has already taken place. There is, moreover, no law which prevents Germans from emigrating where they please; and there is no law which prevents France and Austria from supplying Maximilian with all the material of war he may demand. The truth is that the liberals, unless they receive assistance, must depend upon their own good swords for some time yet. It is but justice, however, that they should receive assistance, and that, too, from our Government. We have long enough nursed the selfish policy of non-intervention in the affairs of the Spanish-American Republics; long enough seen them browbeaten and plundered by monarchical Europe, which has taken advantage of our selfishness in forcing all the struggling republics to the south of us from enjoying any ray of light from us excepting that which has given them their revolutionary impetus. Sisters in a common cause, we have acted most unkindly towards them, and the results we every day witness in such acts as the invasion of Mexico, and the bullying of the whole Pacific coast by Spain, which, the news just reaches us, has added the appendix to the long list of horrors which, through her hands, have cursed Spanish-America, by the disgraceful bombardment of Valparaiso. Surely we lack generosity, surely we are without common humanity even, if we permit these constant and glaring outrages upon a people who are struggling to raise their heads above the inherited curses of Europe. Even in a selfish point of view the benefits which we might reap in throwing a protecting influence over Spanish-America would more than repay all warfare which we might have to wage on their account; for, once be it known that we stood as the champion of justice between them and the European nations, there would be no causes given for any active interference. The nation that lives entirely for itself can make but a poor mark in the history of the world, and the jingle of its money bags will scarcely throw its echoes so far into the future as would the broad policy of protection to human progress.

France recognizes the government of Maximilian as the legitimate ruling power of Mexico; we recognize that of the liberals, under Juarez. France is not making war against Mexico, but is furnishing troops to what she calls the legitimate government, for a stipulated price according to a written contract. Now, if France has the right to furnish the government which she recognizes with mercenary troops and money to carry on the war—and this right is recognized in Europe by other governments—why have we not a similar legitimate right to furnish war *materiel* and cash to the government which we recognize? The liberals are not in want of men. They could to-day raise an army of three hundred thousand had they the means for supplying it with munitions of war. They want money, and we as a people would only be doing them and their cause simple justice were we to furnish it to them in whatever quantities may be required. We do not advocate this course that we may gain any foothold in the Northern provinces of Mexico, for we have quite territory enough to suit the mass of the American people; although there be many who have made large investments in Sonora with the hope that the schemes of President Buchanan, in 1859, might redound to the advantage of those who were in the secret. These men are now willing to argue for any government which promises stability, without reference to its principles. We believe, however, that their only hope of stability in the Northern provinces, unless they are annexed to the United States, is in the liberal government, for they will assuredly be the battle ground of the contending parties until Maximilian is driven from the country.

The present condition of Mexico is scarcely changed from what it was at the first occupation of the French troops and the crowning of Maximilian. The Emperor can scarcely travel five miles in any direction without a large escort, as a protection against the guerrilla bands, which keep the foreign troops constantly employed, even in the most pacified districts. Of the war in the Northern provinces, we hear the most conflicting accounts; but judging even from those most in favor of the Imperialists, they are waging an exhaustive warfare against the large and constantly increasing forces of the liberals, who appear to be rapidly gaining ground.

The *Pall Mall Gazette* of March 9, 1865, says :—" It looks as if we might hope for peace and civilization when there are no more Mexicans." Mexico had her dawn of civilization and peace at the very moment that France invaded her soil in 1862, and the true hope for her is when there are no more foreign bayonets upon her soil to thrust her back into the darkness from which she had just emerged. From calculations made from official dispatches, published in the Mexican imperial journals, it appears that there took place, during the year 1865, three hundred and twenty-two encounters of arms, or about on an average, a battle or a skirmish for every day in the year. Is Mexico under control of Maximilian or the liberalists?

The war which has been waged by the French troops is in no manner superior in character to that civil warfare which was in Europe so much condemned before the landing of a foreign force. The mercenaries of Maximilian have, if we may believe all accounts, been as rigorously cruel in their treatment of the Mexicans opposed to them as ever England was in the treatment of the Sepoy troops during the East India rebellion. The barbarous order of Maximilian, in October, 1865, to mercilessly shoot down all liberals found under arms shows not only how hard the imperial forces have been pressed, but also the sanguinary character of the struggle which they are forced to maintain to preserve even a show of European-reflected royalty upon the soil which had been so dishonorably usurped. The liberals are, however, fast effecting the recovery of the country. This is shown by the fact that the battles are constantly increasing in number, and that where there was one battle in the opening of 1865, there are now two. No quarter has been the rule of warfare, and the result has been a terrible loss of life on both sides. The desperate resolve of the Mexicans to free their soil from the invader makes the task of the latter to pacify the country almost a hopeless one, while the "moral support" which the Emperor Napoleon furnishes to the government he has so generously permitted the Mexican people to unanimously choose, is fast losing ground before the sturdy blows of a people who prefer the enshrinement of a different kind of morality upon their political altars.

From reliable information the imperial treasury of Maximilian is almost as hard pushed for funds as was that of the liberals when the invaders first landed. It appears that they have already been obliged to resort to that plan to which their predecessors in power have been forced before them—the selling of the orders of the Minister of Finance on the Custom Houses at a discount—to obtain means to meet the demands on the Treasury. There is but one hope. Maximilian again turns his eyes towards Napoleon, and Napoleon towards the French people. Will the latter, already depleted in purse by this heavy drain in support of an idea, again respond, and aid the Mexican Imperialists in the formation of a foreign legion with which to continue their policy of Mexican pacification?

SUPPLEMENT.

Successes of the Liberals—Maximilian grossly Deceived—Financial condition of the Country—Church Party with Santa Anna again in the Field—Effects of the Invasion—Dispute about the Presidency — Grant of Extraordinary Powers to Juarez—Mexico fights the Republican Battle for the whole Continent—Concluding Remarks.

The late information from Mexico informs us that the so-called empire is tottering to its fall; and yet, we believe that efforts will be made to maintain it in the face of every obstacle; the liberals are, however, overrunning the whole country, and the strong strategic positions of the various States are rapidly falling into their hands. Were the Emperor Napoleon famed for his honor, we might anticipate some new move in favor of the unfortunate prince Maximilian, to whom he has presented a "sacred white elephant;" but we are too well instructed in his history to believe that the man who could approve of perfidy in the first act at La Soledad, can blush at the desertion of the archduke in the present condition of the tragic-comedy called the Empire. As we have before remarked, European complications may be necessary to gloss over the failure; and there is more of Mexico to-day in the present hostile attitude of the great powers of Europe, than is seen upon the surface.

The archduke Maximilian was grossly deceived by all parties, as to the condition of Mexico, before he crossed the Atlantic. The misrepresentations of the interested European powers were only made patent to him when he found that the part of Mexico which he governed was only ruled under the gleam of foreign bayonets: and yet it appears that, in the treaty which he made wi h Napoleon III., for the retention of a whole *corps d' armée*, he was somewhat doubtful of the truth of the picture of Mexico which the clergy photographed upon the the monarchical retina of Europe. Perhaps he even distrusted the truthfulness of Santa Anna's words, who, on the 22d December, 1863, wrote to him—"I may also assure your Imperial Highness that the voice raised in Mexico to proclaim your respected name is not the voice of a party. An immense majority of the nation desire to restore the empire of the Montezumas with your Imperial Highness at its head, believing it to be the only remedy for existing ills, and the ultimate anchor of its hopes."

The financial condition of the so-called empire is to-day worse than that of any party which ever occupied the capital during any revolutionary overturning in the country. The so-called empire has attempted to load Mexico with a mountain of debt, many times exceeding that which the nation owed in 1861; while the immense increase of expenditures for this bastard government compares very unfavorably with the more democratic outlays for the support of republican institutions.

Up to January 1st, 1866, official data, published at Washington, shows:

First. That France has charged to Mexico for expenses of invasion to July 1st, 1864.. $50,000,000

Second. That loans have been negotiated for Maximilian in France, amounting to... 150,000,000

Third. That the claims of France, admitted by the constitutional government before the intervention, were only............ 2,859,917

Fourth. That the French claims recognized by Maximilian already amount to........ 192,962,962

We have also the following

COMPARISONS.

Foreign debt, as attempted to be recognized by Maximilian................. .... $271,735,605
Foreign debt, as recognized by the constitutional government....................... 81,632,560

Attempted increase by Maximilian........ $190,103,045

Annual interest required to be paid by Maximilian............................ $12,966,204
Annual interest under the government of the Republic............................ 2,760,022

Attempted increase by Maximilian....... $10,206,182

Annual expenditures under Maximilian...... $49,929,326
Annual expenditures, fixed by the national Congress, under the Republic.......... 11,087,440

Annual increase under Maximilian....... $38,841,886

Annual salary of Maximilian, so called Emperor of Mexico..................... $1,500,000
Annual salary of the President of the Republic. 30,000

It will be here noticed that *the interest alone*, which is required to be paid by Maximilian, *exceeds* by *almost two millions of dollars the total annual expenditures sanctioned by the constitutional Congress, before the invasion.*

The result of these considerations shows with severity against the attempted foisting of a monarchical government upon the country. To make this indebtedness good, there is a combination of a powerful moneyed interest to uphold the empire, upon which they put almost their total dependence for future payment of claims. This moncyed interest is very nearly equal in amount, although not equal in power, to that which the church held, while for so many years it contested the rights of cash against high political principles. In support of the empire there is also a considerable party of Mexicans who embarked their fortunes in it; others who have received titles and distinctions under it; others who have grown rich from its contracts; others who have entered the country from foreign lands and accepted from it peculiar and valuable privileges; all combined forming a powerful party, not entirely to be ignored, even after the *promised* withdrawal of the French troops. But we believe that the postponement of this withdrawal to so late a date, is to give all these interests time to consolidate, with the hope also, that, in eighteen months, the additional interests that may be brought to work in harmony with the others, may enable the imperial government to make head against all opponents. In view of this, we question the wisdom of our government in allowing the longer continuance of this bastard usurpation of the rights of a people, and the enduring of this standing insult to the whole Western continent.

The church party are also in the field with new political combinations, with the hope that, by some extraordinary turn of fortune, they may regain some of their lost power, and re-establish a reactionary government in place of that to which they betrayed their country, and which in turn betrayed them. Again, as of old, their exponent is Santa Anna; and this retrogressive champion issues a *pronunciamiento*,* crying "Down with the empire!"—*which he helped establish*—and "Long live the republic!" — *which he helped overthrow.* The clergy, with the hope of driving from the soil the power which has broken faith with them, are now making one grand rally to free themselves from its weight; therefore they cry Union of all parties and all political creeds, but they want Union and the Leadership; this, we believe,

---

* See New York Herald, June 14, 1866.

would be ruin to the liberal cause, and we see in it, therefore, the reasons for the distrust with which all the liberals look at the attempted foisting of Santa Anna upon the republican platform. The clergy, finding that they cannot establish a church party, and that intervention and monarchy fail to drown the the republic in their waves, very naturally seek for a footing under the republican standard, and demand a position which it would be fatal for the liberals to grant them.

Growing out of French invasion and the consequent distracted condition of the country, there are other combinations in the field derogatory to the true interests of Mexican civilization and progress. Among these has been the inability of the Mexican people to hold a constitutional election for President before the expiration of the late presidential term. The result has been that, by virtue of the constitution, General Ortega, as "President of the Supreme Court of Justice," considered himself entitled, on the 1st December, 1865, to the presidential chair. On that date, however, he was absent from the country, and, therefore, could not assume the duties of the office. He had claimed that he was entitled to the seat in 1864; but the decision of the cabinet was against him, and to this he apparently acquiesced like a true patriot.

It is easy to sit quietly in one's study and render a decision of what is the right in time of peace; but in time of great public peril, when, by civil commotion, by foreign invasion, and by a struggle that saps the life-blood of a nation, the whole conditions of the problem become changed, a point at least should be yielded to that stern military law which is the growth of the moment, and which, unwritten, is still to be considered when the destinies of a people perhaps hang upon the firmness of the hand that presses the helm. A true patriot never leaves his post at that moment, no matter what personal considerations may influence him.

It is not within our province to decide the question of Ortega's right to the presidency, but we believe that a strict rendering of military law would cause his arrest for desertion and trial by court martial were he to return to Mexico; for, nearly twelve months previous to the time at which the cabinet of Juarez decided that the presidential term should be extended, General Ortega applied for, and received from his government, a "leave of transit" from Chihuahua through the United States to another part of Mexico, for the purpose of organizing some military expedition against the enemy. Ever since this leave was granted Ortega has been in the United States. Instead of standing beside the other heroes of Mexico who have so bravely fought in the cause of freedom, he has apparently deserted the cause of his country. General Ortega is a brave man, with many good qualities of head and heart; but his place was by the side of Juarez, battling for the overthrow of the empire, that, in case of the death of the latter, he might take up the standard and continue the contest. Should Juarez die, there is no one to fill the chair, according to the letter of the constitution, unless, by virtue of the powers vested in him by the National Congress, he has appointed some one. The decrees of Congress, for this and every purpose, have been more than ample, and show what confidence has been centered in the present incumbent of the presidential chair. On December 11, 1861, Congress granted extraordinary powers to the President, only limiting him to the preservation of the national territory and the independence of the country intact, and the support of the constitution. On December 13, 1861, a supplementary article was added, even granting power "to conclude treaties and conventions, and place them in the course of execution." Again, May 3, 1862, and October 27, 1862, and still again May 27, 1863, Congress reconfirmed these extraordinary powers to the President, who, on the 8th Nov., 1865, by their virtue, issued a decree extending his term of office, and also that of the "President of the Supreme Court of Justice," until "the condition of the war may permit an election to be constitutionally held."

Besides the reasons given in this decree for the extension, there were other and powerful ones, born of the situation and potent in their solution of the contest against the invaders of the soil. It was a case of imperious necessity that Juarez should continue to govern; for, it was his government that the French proclaimed war against, and not against the Mexican people who had with an overwhelming majority placed him in the presidential chair. The wish of every true Mexican was, therefore, that the man of their choice should remain at the head of their government, in the face of all foreign opposition; providing that, in addition to this wish, there were good and sufficient constitutional reasons for his so doing. In this view then, Juarez represents the will of Mexico in opposition to the will of France. It was, moreover, necessary to have a sterling man in the position, that required a persistent, unwavering purpose, with unfaltering nerve, to wage a contest of years against the bastard empire of Maximilian! Fortunate has it been for Mexico that she found the man whose sterling integrity was proof against all the dazzling allurements of the empire; who could not be bought, nor yet deceived; whose sole purpose of life appears to be to free his country from her invaders, and restore the cause of order and civilization which foreign intervention so rudely hurled aside, at the moment it was established, after the terrific battle of half a century.

The attempt of France to overthrow the government of the people has, thus far, been unsuccessful, and it should be the effort to-day of every real Mexican patriot to prevent the machinations of the French Emperor from establishing any government in place of the present liberal one whereby, upon the exodus of Maximilian, he may be able to attach to the Mexican national debt the long and unfortunate bill he has contracted in his foolish attempt to establish an empire in the heart of the Western Republican World!

Mexico is to-day fighting the great battle of republicanism against imperialism. The direct insult which France offered to the Mexican people, in the attempt to establish *a government not of their choice*, is also an indirect insult to every republic on this continent, and most of all to the United States. The conquest of Mexico was to be a foothold for the propagandism of monarchical ideas in the New World. One after the other the republics were to fall until human liberty and republicanism became a transient bubble of the past, that showed its bright colors in the sunshine, but burst at the first blast; but the wave of imperialism has broken against a rock; lashed into foam, it hurls itself in vain against an unaided and poverty-stricken republic which fifty years of civil strife have torn and wounded to the heart. Shame! shame! that we, as a people, look on quietly and see Mexico fight the battle of both North and South America. Shame! to the Great Republic that we bind our sympathies in the shroud of selfishness and see imperial Europe scourge, without cause, the young republics to the south of us, who, just struggling into the light of civilization, are baffled and thrown back into the past because the Colossus of the North lies dead to their appeals against a common enemy.

With the overthrow of Maximilian, there will naturally arise new complications, born of the evils which have dropped from the folds of the French flag. The whole political atmosphere, driven into cloud and whirlwind by the invasion, will not settle into calm under the first ray of sunshine.

Our own civil war, and its present phase, should teach us to have patience with a people whose political fortunes have been stirred to more tragic action by five decades of contest and the solution of a dozen curses in its one great crucible of revolution. Grant them a few years to restore their country!—first,

www.ingramcontent.com/pod-product-compliance
Lightning Source LLC
Chambersburg PA
CBHW020325090426
42735CB00009B/1412